CARIBBEANCOCKTAILS

FOOD AND DRINK PHOTOGRAPHY BY KRISTEN BROCHMANN

CARIBBEAN COCKTAILS

JENNIFER**TRAINER**THOMPSON

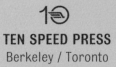

TEN SPEED PRESS
Berkeley / Toronto

1🕊️

Ten Speed Press
P.O. Box 7123
Berkeley, California 94707

Distributed in Australia by Simon and Schuster Australia, in Canada by Ten Speed Press Canada, in New Zealand by Southern Publishers Group, in South Africa by Real Books, in Southeast Asia by Berkeley Books, and in the United Kingdom and Europe by Airlift Book Company.

NOTE: *One of the recipes in this book includes raw fish. When fish is consumed raw, there is always the risk that bacteria may be present. For this reason, always buy the freshest fish available from a reliable fishmonger, storing it in the refrigerator until it is served. Because of health risks associated with the consumption of bacteria that can be present in raw fish, these foods should not be consumed by infants, small children, pregnant women, the elderly, or any people who may be immunocompromised.*

Cover and interior design by Betsy Stromberg
Principal photography by Kristen Brochmann
Other photography (pages vi, 27, 61, 70) by Robert Holmes;
    (pages 20,126–127, 128–129) by Jennifer Trainer Thompson; (page 42) by Doug Carver;
    (page 76) by Scott Doggett.

Library of Congress Cataloging-in-Publication Data

Thompson, Jennifer Trainer.
  Caribbean cocktails / Jennifer Trainer Thompson ; food and drink
photography by Kristen Brochmann.
      p. cm.
Includes bibliographical references and index.
  ISBN 1-58008-364-1 (pbk.)
  1. Cocktails. I. Title.
  TX951 .T482 2003
  641.8'74--dc21
                              2002015043

First printing, 2003

Printed in China

1 2 3 4 5 6 7 8 9 10 — 08 07 06 05 04 03

DEDICATION

To Big Joe, who introduced me to piña coladas on the top deck in Vieques, and who considers cocktails a higher art form.

ACKNOWLEDGMENTS

A big tropical toast to Dennis Hayes, who never wants credit but is a driving force behind this book (and Ten Speed Press), and whose affection for rum, sun, and the spirit of the islands runs deep.

A heartfelt thanks, too, to Nancy Thomas, especially, and also Linda Stripp, Shane Armstrong, Chris Tolar, and Jody Fijal, who helped capture the flavors of the Caribbean, and to photographer Kristen Brochmann, with whom I've logged a few nautical miles. I'm grateful, too, for the input of James Weis and Inn on the Blue Horizon, Ed Batres, Amanda Chilson, Carolyn Beaudreau, Annie Nelson, Eric Kerns, and Doug Carver.

CONTENTS

INTRODUCTION

The first time I saw the islands was during a boat delivery from Mount Desert Island, Maine, to Virgin Gorda. Leaving port on a blustery October morning with woolen hats and down vests, we channeled our way down the Atlantic Intracoastal Waterway, exchanging our down jackets for T-shirts as we headed south. We waited out a hurricane in West Palm Beach, then made a beeline for the Bahamas. Two days out our mast stay broke, which forced us to land on a tiny Bahamian island known on some maps as San Salvador.

The main claim to fame of San Salvador (population 486) is that it's where Columbus first landed in 1492 in his search for the East Indies. Of more immediate interest to our crew (other than hot showers) was the fact that near the beach was a thatched dirt-floor bar that served glorious rum punches. Who cared if we were marooned? (A good thing, too, since we later discovered that it would take a week for the parts to arrive.)

During that week we became aficionados of those rum punches. Jimmy Buffett aptly calls them "boat drinks"—frothy, pastel-colored cocktails with big flavor and often big alcohol. They are more than drinks, they are an attitude; and even if you've never been to the Caribbean, they will take you there. The suggestive power of taste is strong: with a few sips you can see the aquamarine waters, feel the gentle breeze, and start swaying like a palm frond. These drinks transport you.

While some Caribbean drinks are made with tequila and other spirits, the driving force is typically rum, and it is inextricably linked to the history of the Caribbean littoral, which stretches from Key West to Venezuela. Both the drinks and the foods of the Caribbean are fascinating, with each island's specialties combining colonial and native influences. The Caribbean kitchen is eclectic, with obvious African, Asian, British, Spanish, Indian, French, and Dutch touches. You can take a culinary world trip in these turquoise waters—it's a true melting pot.

After Columbus realized that the islands he had encountered were not part of the Orient he sought, he proclaimed them the "West" Indies. He found the indigenous people gentle—he hadn't met the fierce and sometimes cannibalistic Caribs yet—and wrote home that they were perfect for Christianizing and enslaving. (When natives resisted Spanish explorers, they were slaughtered, and slaves were imported from West Africa to replace them. During the 1500s, native tribes became extinct in Cuba.)

On his second voyage in 1493, Columbus brought sugarcane from the Far East (via the Canary Islands) to Hispaniola, the island that is now Haiti and the Dominican Republic. It thrived in the tropical climate, and to meet the huge demand for refined sugar in Europe, soon the English, Spanish, Portuguese, French, and Dutch were establishing island colonies and vast sugar plantations. Sugar mills boiled the cane, which created crystallized sugar and a leftover dark, sticky juice called *melaza* (from Spanish *miel,* "honey") or, in English, molasses.

When mixed with water and left in the hot Caribbean sun, molasses mingles with the natural yeast in the air and ferments. Legend has it that a thirsty slave dipped his spoon into the molasses sludge and discovered rum. By 1650, rum was being produced, the early nickname for it being Kill Devil, because it was thought to be a "cure for Satan's ills." A 1651 manuscript from Barbados notes, "The chief fuddling they make in the island is Rumbullion, alias Kill-Divil, and this is made of sugar canes distilled, a hot, hellish, and terrible liquor." Many plantation owners built rum distilleries next to their sugar refineries so they could produce both sugar and rum. Hundreds of thousands of West Africans were imported as slaves to work the plantations.

Rum was big business. In the early 1600s, the Spanish had ruled the Caribbean, but as the sugar and rum trades (along with cotton, coffee, and tobacco) came to dominate the European economy in the late 1600s and 1700s, other nations coveted the market. Piracy became common, as nations and adventurers fought for control over the islands as well as the schooners bound home loaded with gold, tobacco, rum, and spices.

Interestingly, there were shades of definition of what constituted a pirate. A buccaneer was one kind: an unscrupulous adventurer who preyed on Spanish ships and settlements in the West Indies during the seventeenth century.

Privateers, by contrast, were commissioned by governments to raid ships and colonial outposts bearing the flag of an enemy nation (and they often committed piracy privately while off duty). The Spanish, who sought to claim the New World for their own, thought nothing of capturing British or other European ships and enslaving the crews (and vice versa, since each nation's future depended on its ability to expand trade zones).

The territory was worth fighting over; in England, rum was the number one import (replacing gin as the preferred alcohol in the 1700s), and in the American colonies, rum was also the spirit of choice, with each tavern serving a specialty rum punch. "If the ancients drank wine as our people drink rum and cider," groused John Adams, "it is no wonder we hear of so many possessed with devils." Rum was a form of currency—sailors got paid in rum, slaves were sold for rum. Nearly every Caribbean island had its own rum distillery, and there were many in New England, too—sixty-three in Massachusetts alone in 1750. The northern colonies were part of the infamous Triangular Trade of slaves, rum, and molasses (along with other goods) among New England, the Caribbean, and West Africa.

Captain Barney Hicks of southeastern Massachusetts was typical: he'd go to the Congo with rum, pick up slaves, take them to Santo Domingo and trade them for molasses (his heirs have documented forty-five voyages), then take the molasses up to Newport to make rum and keep the taverns supplied. During the Revolution, he became a privateer and raided British ships. Captured by a British ship that was wrecked off the coast of New Jersey, he was the only survivor (along with the ship's dog), though he lost a leg. His descendants still have two of his wooden legs: one leather-bound (for Sundays), and an "ordinary" wooden leg he used for working around the farm.

By the 1800s, rum production was declining. Trade was disrupted after the American Revolution, and as North American settlers moved to the Midwest and started growing corn, rye, and wheat, whiskey came to be preferred. Rum flourished again during Prohibition, when Americans flocked to Cuba to drink it, breaking through "Rum Row" (the dry zone that extended twelve miles off the coast). "Rum" flights were offered between Florida and Cuba, and steamships sold one-night trips. In the '20s, Cuba became the cocktail capital of the world.

During World War II, rum sales soared by 400 percent; gin and whiskey were in short supply—most distilleries were producing industrial alcohol ("cocktails for Hitler")—and Rum and Cola was the number one drink, inspired no doubt by the Andrews Sisters' wartime hit song of the same name about American GIs dallying with hookers in Trinidad. Americans looked south to the littoral for inspiration, and discovered tequila and rum. Trader Vic mixed his first Mai Tai in 1944, and the tropical craze was set in motion.

By the 1960s, rum was passé (except for college beach parties in Fort Lauderdale or Caribbean vacations), and over the subsequent decades preppies, then yuppies, preferred single malt scotches, microbrewed beers, and flavored vodkas. The '60s and '70s also saw an explosion of tourism in the Caribbean, followed by new settlers (sailors, expats, and hippies) who introduced french fries, pizza, and cheeseburgers to paradise. Someone forgot to tell the folks in the Caribbean that rum wasn't cool, but who wants a Macallan twelve-year-old Scotch under a palm tree anyway?

Today, rum—dusting off its reputation as rustic, crude, and a bit collegiate—is once again flourishing (Bacardi alone sells more than twenty million cases a year), and aficionados are discovering what islanders have known for years: this spirit is not only delicious for mixing but, when aged in oak casks, is exquisite served neat and can compete with fine Ports and Scotches. It's no coincidence that Cadenhead, a Scottish lowland single-malt whiskey merchant, also bottles Demerara rum.

To get you going "tropo," there's a Caribbean Cocktails Reading Room on page 128, since rum and drinking in the islands are the stuff of writers, pirates, colonial splendor, and fantasy. Check out the people who wrote about the West Indies, from Robert Louis Stevenson to Hemingway. For a more visual approach to getting in the spirit, consult Caribbean Cocktails Movies on page 126. And to set it all in motion, enjoy the music references throughout, which range from popular to obscure. I dare anyone to enjoy a rum punch while listening to "Hot Hot Hot" and not be transported to your favorite beach (either in your memory or in your fantasy).

—Jennifer Trainer Thompson
Vieques, November 2002

CARIBBEANBAR ESSENTIALS

SPIRITS

Blue curaçao

Gin

Kahlúa

Lillet Blanc

Midori (melon liqueur)

Rum (white, gold, dark, and spiced)

Tequila: an affordable one, plus an expensive one such as El Tesoro or Chinaco Blanco

Tia Maria

Triple Sec

Vodka

SPIRITED BUT NONALCOHOLIC

Angostura bitters

Club soda

Coconut milk

Cola

Cranberry juice cocktail

Cream of coconut

Grapefruit juice

Grenadine

Lemons and limes

Mint (fresh)

Nutmeg (whole)

Passion fruit syrup

Pineapple juice

Sour mix

Tonic

SIZE MATTERS

WINE	COLLINS	CHAMPAGNE	SHERRY/CORDIAL	MARTINI	OLD-FASHIONED
	(a.k.a. highball, for drinks over ice with flat or fizzy water)				(stout and sturdy tumbler)

BAR EQUIPMENT

Blender

Jigger

Juicer (always use fresh lemon and lime juices)

Cocktail shaker (get one that holds at least 14 ounces so it can shake two drinks; some varieties come with a strainer), preferably metal

Strainer (if you, like James Bond, like it neat—i.e., you don't want ice—and you don't have a shaker, you might want to invest in a Hawthorn strainer, the kind with the spring around the rim)

NOTES ON INGREDIENTS

Lemons and limes: Pick heavy fruit, which will be the juiciest. Release the lime's juices by rolling it before cutting. Key limes are small (the size of a golf ball), with a thin skin that's yellower than that of American limes (which are a hybrid of the Key lime and the citron).

Coconut: The fruit of a coconut palm, a coconut has a woody shell that is encased in a fibrous husk. (Coconuts that you find in stores usually have the husk removed.) Young coconuts have fresh meat and an edible jelly-like coating between the meat and the liquid. The meat dries out as the coconut gets older. To crack a coconut, either whack it with a hammer or the blunt side of a cleaver, or heat it for ten minutes in a 300°F oven, then crack the shell and pry out the meat. Have a bowl handy to capture the liquid.

Coconut milk: Coconut milk can be found canned in most grocery stores in the Asian foods section. (Or make your own: pour 1 cup of boiling water or milk over 2 cups of grated fresh coconut, then strain after half an hour.) Coconut milk is used in curries, sauces, and stews. Don't confuse it with cream of coconut (Coco López is a popular brand), which is a sweet, thick cream (like a syrup) used in drinks such as piña coladas.

Nutmeg: Buy it whole and grate as needed. Grated fresh nutmeg is so aromatic and strong that it transforms a frothy coconut drink.

Ice: Watery ice makes a poor drink. Take ice out of the freezer just before making your drink. If using a metal cocktail shaker, fill the shaker with ice and ingredients and shake until a frost appears on the blender (about fifteen seconds); longer than that will result in a watery drink, and shorter than that won't chill the drink adequately.

RUMDRINKS

When people think of Caribbean drinks, they think first of rum. Rum is distilled from sugarcane (cane syrup, cane juice, or molasses), which gives this liquor an underlying sweetness. The color is determined by three factors: the distillation process (lighter rums are made in "continuous" stills, but darker premium rums are often made in old-fashioned pot stills); the aging process (some rums are aged in oak or bourbon barrels for up to twenty years); and in some cases, the addition of flavorings such as sherry, caramel, or raisins, or of colorings. In broad terms, English- and French-influenced islands tend to produce dark rums, while Spanish-influenced islands favor white or light rums.

There are four basic types of rum. **WHITE** or light rums are clear like water, light-tasting, and good in mixed drinks or punches. **GOLDEN** or medium rums are aged in oak barrels, which give them a slightly spicy aroma. They have a softly sweet aftertaste, and are appropriate in cocktails in which you'd like the rum flavor to be evident. Full-bodied, somewhat spicy **DARK** rums are good for mixing when you want a predominant rum flavor. They're also terrific served neat, as you would a Port, or simply with a bit of ice. (Vintage rums distilled in small batches are particularly rich and aromatic.)

Finally, **SPICED** rums are white, golden, or dark rums infused with spices, citrus, vanilla, or other flavorings. They work well with fruit; in grogs, punches, and mixed drinks; and as a cooking ingredient. Some people like to take their spiced rums straight, too.

You can also find rum infused with coconut. Some foodies snub such a concoction, but it can make a damned good tropical drink.

BOATDRINK

SERVES 1

This fruity tropical drink will put you on island time. Be as liberal as you desire with the rum. Always use fresh sour mix, which is easy to make (see the recipe below).

> 1 ounce freshly squeezed orange juice
> 2 ounces pineapple juice
> 1 teaspoon grenadine
> $1^1/2$ ounces white rum
> 1 ounce Captain Morgan's Spiced Rum or other spiced rum
> 1 ounce sour mix (below)
> $^1/2$ ounce Triple Sec
> Maraschino cherry, for garnish

Fill a tall glass with ice. Pour the orange juice, pineapple juice, grenadine, white rum, spiced rum, sour mix, and Triple Sec into the glass and stir gently. Garnish with the cherry.

Recommended Listening

"Boat Drinks," by Jimmy Buffett, from *Volcano*

Sour Mix

To make a batch of sour mix, combine 1 12-ounce can of frozen lemonade concentrate with 2 12-ounce cans of frozen limeade concentrate, then use the empty container to add 6 12-ounce cans' worth of water. Keep covered, in the refrigerator.

APOCALYPSO

SERVES 1

Originating in Trinidad centuries ago, calypso music was to the West Indies what spirituals were to the South: a vehicle for the oppressed to sing their woes and transfer information in a lyrical, clandestine manner.

**2 ounces Mount Gay Barbados Rum
or other golden rum**

1 teaspoon grenadine

1 tablespoon freshly squeezed lemon juice

4 ounces pineapple juice

Splash of ginger ale

Pineapple wedge, for garnish

Fill a large Collins glass with ice. Add the rum, grenadine, lemon juice, pineapple juice, and ginger ale in order and stir. Garnish with the pineapple wedge.

Recommended Listening

"Oh Goody!" by Barefoot, from *Hot! Hot! Hot! Collection*

"Calypso is a thing I'm telling you
When you are singing, you must learn to impromptu
Never mind your English, but mind your rhymes,
When you get the gist of it, just sing in time,
For veteran calypsonians are known to be
Men who can sing on anything instantaneously."
—The Gorilla (calypsonian)

RUMPUNCH

SERVES A CROWD

Every island bar has a version of this famous Caribbean drink. I've sipped some great ones—on the veranda at the Cotton House on Mustique and in the open-air bar at Bananas on Vieques, to name a few. This recipe follows the ditty: "One of sour, two of sweet, three of strong, and four of weak." A "topping" layer of dark rum, coupled with a short straw, will bring the aromatic magic of rum to the fore.

> 1 part lime juice
> 2 parts grenadine, or simple syrup (page 24) or a combination
> 3 parts rum; either white, golden, or dark or a mixture
> 4 parts fruit juices (pineapple, orange, passion fruit, guava, mango)
> Freshly grated nutmeg, for garnish
> Lime slices, for garnish

Mix the lime juice, syrup, rum, and fruit juices in a large bowl. Sprinkle with nutmeg and lime. To serve, ladle the punch into ice-filled glasses.

Recommended Listening

"Dance Bonne Pa Dance," by Kanda Bongo Man, from *Hurricane Zouk*

MOJITO

SERVES 1

This classic Cuban drink (pronounced *mo-HEE-to*) is all about the fragrant mint mingling with the rum, lime, and sugar.

$^1/_2$ to 1 teaspoon powdered (or regular) sugar
$^1/_2$ lime, freshly squeezed
4 peppermint leaves plus 1 sprig, for garnish
2 ounces white rum
1 ounce club soda (optional)

Put the sugar in a highball glass and squeeze in the lime juice; stir to dissolve. Add the mint leaves and crush against the side of the glass until the aromatic oils are released. Add the lime rind. Fill the glass with crushed ice, add the rum. Top with club soda. Garnish with the mint sprig.

NOTE: *A refreshing cooler, mojitos are fun at parties. To make a pitcher, multiply the ingredient quantities by the number of guests. Mash the mint and sugar in a bowl with a wooden spoon (or in a mortar with a pestle), then add the lime juice and rum and stir until the sugar dissolves. Strain the mixture into a pitcher. (The recipe can be made up to this point several hours ahead and kept refrigerated.) When ready to serve, stir gently, and pour the mixture into glasses filled with crushed ice. Top it off with club soda, if desired (it's not authentic, but the effervescence of sparkling water is nice), and serve with a sprig of mint and a wedge of lime as garnishes.*

Recommended Listening

"Sweet Rum and Starlight," by Earl Klugh, from *Love Songs*

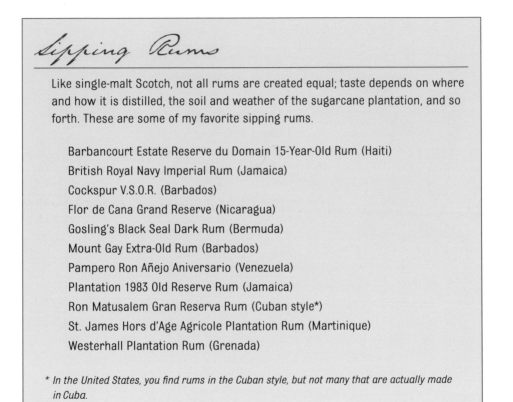

Sipping Rums

Like single-malt Scotch, not all rums are created equal; taste depends on where and how it is distilled, the soil and weather of the sugarcane plantation, and so forth. These are some of my favorite sipping rums.

Barbancourt Estate Reserve du Domain 15-Year-Old Rum (Haiti)

British Royal Navy Imperial Rum (Jamaica)

Cockspur V.S.O.R. (Barbados)

Flor de Cana Grand Reserve (Nicaragua)

Gosling's Black Seal Dark Rum (Bermuda)

Mount Gay Extra-Old Rum (Barbados)

Pampero Ron Añejo Aniversario (Venezuela)

Plantation 1983 Old Reserve Rum (Jamaica)

Ron Matusalem Gran Reserva Rum (Cuban style*)

St. James Hors d'Age Agricole Plantation Rum (Martinique)

Westerhall Plantation Rum (Grenada)

* In the United States, you find rums in the Cuban style, but not many that are actually made in Cuba.

ELPRESIDENTE

SERVES 2

This Cuban drink was named after General Menocal, who in the '30s liked rum almost as much as power. This drink is traditionally made with Bacardi, though other white rums may be substituted.

2 ounces Bacardi white rum
1 ounce dry vermouth
2 ounces pineapple juice
$1/2$ ounce grenadine
1 ounce sour mix (page 10)
Lime slice, for garnish

Fill a mixing glass or cocktail shaker with ice and add the rum, vermouth, pineapple juice, grenadine, and sour mix. Shake well and strain into an attractive martini-style glass. Garnish with a lime slice.

Recommended Listening

"Mimi," by Cubanissimo, from *Reincarnación*

Originally produced in Cuba by Desi Arnaz's grandfather, Bacardi rum moved its operations to Puerto Rico after Fidel Castro nationalized the rum industry and confiscated the company's plant in 1960. Today, Puerto Rico remains the world's largest rum producer—mostly because, as a commonwealth of the United States, Puerto Rico can ship its products to the States duty-free.

CUBALIBRE

SERVES 1

A far cry from the pedestrian Rum and Cola, this elegant libation was invented by one of Teddy Roosevelt's Rough Riders fighting the Spanish-American War in Cuba, who asked a Havana bartender to mix him a cocktail of rum with cola and a bit of lime on ice. (Created fourteen years before, Coca-Cola was considered exotic and was brought to Cuba by Americans.) Other soldiers asked for the same drink, and they toasted the locals and their victory—*"Cuba libre!"* ("Free Cuba!").

> **2 ounces white rum (Bacardi is traditional)**
> **$1/4$ lime**
> **1 to $1^1/2$ ounces cola (to taste)**

Fill a highball glass with ice. Add the rum; squeeze in the lime juice, then toss in the rind. Add the cola and stir.

Recommended Listening

"Rum and Coca-Cola," sung by the Andrews Sisters; or by Lord Invader, from *1946 Calypso at Midnight*

"If you ever go down Trinidad
They make you feel so very glad
Calypso sing and make up rhyme
Guarantee you one real good time
Drinkin' rum and Coca-Cola, go down Point Cumana
Both mother and daughter, working for the Yankee dollar
Oh, beat it man, beat it."

—from "Rum and Coca-Cola"

LATIN LEMONADE

SERVES 1

Flavored with coconut, Malibu Caribbean Rum seems a bit cheesy, and it *does* smell like suntan lotion, but it offers a deliciously subtle coconut flavor in this grown-up lemonade.

$1^1/_2$ ounces vodka

$1^1/_2$ ounces Malibu Caribbean Rum or other coconut-flavored rum

3 ounces pineapple juice

Maraschino cherry, for garnish

Fill a tall glass with ice and pour the vodka, rum, and pineapple juice over. Stir with a straw. Garnish with the cherry.

Recommended Listening

"The Dolphins," by Fred Neil, from *The Other Side of This Life*

BUCCANEER

SERVES 2

Made with Captain Morgan's Spiced Rum, this buccaneer is sweet and smooth, with a hint of almond and coconut. (The word *buccaneer,* by the way, derives from the practice by French pirates of curing their meat in the native manner, using a wooden frame called a *boucan*. They were first called *boucaniers*.)

$1^1/2$ ounces Malibu Caribbean Rum or other coconut-flavored rum
$1^1/2$ ounces amaretto
$1^1/2$ ounces Captain Morgan's Spiced Rum or other spiced rum
$1^1/2$ ounces cranberry juice cocktail
$1^1/2$ ounces pineapple juice

In a cocktail shaker filled with ice, combine all ingredients. Shake vigorously five times, then strain into two martini glasses or other festive glasses.

Recommended Listening

"A Pirate Looks at Forty," by Jimmy Buffett, from *A1A*

Of all the buccaneers who plied the azure waters, Captain Henry Morgan was perhaps the most infamous, stealing even from his own men. Born in 1635 in Wales, he arrived in Barbados in 1655 with Oliver Cromwell's expedition, and by 1663 was part of a flotilla that plundered forts in Santiago, Cuba and Campeche, Mexico (the forts fell in a day, and the buccaneers took home fourteen Spanish ships as prizes). On his way back to England, he dabbled in a little private pirating in Panama (plundering a fortune in silver, gold, and jewels), knowing full well that England was not at war with Spain. The governor of Jamaica had to slap his wrist by jailing him and shipping him home to England. By the time he arrived, England was feuding with Spain, and King Charles II instead knighted Morgan and sent him back to Jamaica as the lieutenant governor.

FLOAT**YOUR**BOAT

SERVES 1

Float Your Boat is exquisite on a hot night as an after-dinner drink—or even as an apéritif. Captain Morgan's is a Puerto Rican–style rum blended with spices.

$1/2$ ounce brandy

1 ounce Captain Morgan's Spiced Rum,
  or other spiced rum

2 ounces sour mix (page 10)

$1/2$ ounce blue curaçao

Freshly squeezed juice of $1/4$ lime

Lemon wedge or slice, for garnish

Fill a rocks glass with ice. Add the brandy, rum, sour mix, curaçao, and lime juice. Cover with a cocktail shaker and shake five times. Garnish with lemon.

Recommended Listening

"If I Had a Boat," by Lyle Lovett, from *Pontiac*

Pirates were surprisingly democratic; everyone on board had a vote, and the captain was elected. (If he performed poorly, he was thrown overboard or marooned.) Pirates always drew up codes of ethics, which the entire crew signed. The code of Bartholomew Roberts, a religious teetotaler captain who prohibited gambling among his crew and captured more than four hundred ships between 1719 and 1722, is typical.

- All important decisions are to be put to a vote.
- Any man caught stealing shall be marooned.
- All pistols and cutlasses will be kept clean.
- No women are allowed on board.
- Any man who deserts ship in battle shall be put to death.
- All crew quarrels will be settled onshore.
- The captain and quartermaster shall receive two shares of the booty; the master gunner and boatswain, one and a half shares; other officers, one and a quarter shares; all others, one share each.
- Injuries are to be compensated. Any man who loses a limb in battle shall receive extra booty.

Pirates flew a red flag (*joli rouge*, from which *Jolly Roger* is derived) to warn people that if they resisted the pirate ship, their blood would flow. Pirates also created their own flags. Blackbeard—who scared his attackees in the early 1700s by braiding his beard with hemp fuses and then lighting them as he was about to raid, so his beard would smoke as he attacked—selected a flag that featured an hourglass, as a warning to victims that their time was up.

DARK**AND**STORMY

SERVES 1

This thirst-quenching drink is a bit like an alcoholic ginger ale. It's a great refresher after you've been working hard outdoors. Made by a German brewmaster who researched Jamaican methods of brewing ginger ale, Reed's Ginger Beer is sparkling water infused with fresh gingerroot and sweetened with pineapple juice. It has a spicy ginger bite, and it's great on ice.

> $1^1/_2$ **ounces white rum**
> **1 bottle Reed's Ginger Beer**
> **Lime wedge, for garnish**

Fill a 10-ounce glass with ice. Add the rum, top with the ginger beer, and garnish with the lime wedge.

Recommended Listening

"Waiting in Vain," by Bob Marley, from *Exodus;* or by Annie Lenox, from *Waiting in Vain*

Fifteen men on a dead man's chest—
Yo-ho-ho and a bottle of rum.
Drink and the Devil have done for the rest—
Yo-ho-ho and a bottle of rum.
—Robert Louis Stevenson, *Treasure Island* (1883)

BANANARAMA

SERVES 1 OR 2

This drink is a bit like a banana colada. Be sure to use cream of coconut, not coconut milk, to ensure the desired sweet taste and creamy smoothness.

> 9 ounces ice (1 heaping cupful)
> 1 ounce spiced rum
> 1 ounce Coco López (cream of coconut)
> 1 ounce banana liqueur
> 1 ounce pineapple juice
> $^1/_2$ ounce cassis syrup

Place the ice in a blender and add all the remaining ingredients. Blend six seconds. Pour into your favorite glass. Makes one large drink or two small ones.

Recommended Listening

"Coconut Man," by Taj Mahal,
from *Sacred Island*

LETI'PUNCH

SERVES 1

From the French islands of Martinique, Guadeloupe, St. Martin, and St. Bart's, this drink is traditionally served at any time of day, often with a glass of cold water. It's called *décollage* when served in the early morning, *la gazez* when it's a midmorning shot, *ti'goutte* when it's served about eleven, and *ti'punch* just before lunch. As a midafternoon pick-me-up, it's called *l'heure du Christ*, at five o'clock it's *le ti'pape pape,* and at cocktails before dinner it's *ti'punch* again. Use a good rum, as this is a sipping drink.

> **1 teaspoon simple syrup (see below)**
> **$^1/_4$ lime, freshly squeezed**
> **1 to 2 ounces Matusalem or other good-quality rum**

Pour the syrup into a rocks glass and add the lime juice (toss in the rind, too). Stir to blend, then add ice and rum.

NOTE: *You can substitute tropical-fruit syrups for the simple syrup.*

Recommended Listening

"Shakedown Time," by David Rudder, from *Zero*

Simple Syrup

MAKES 1 CUP

Simple syrup—also known as sugar syrup, bar syrup, or rock candy syrup—is a blend of water and sugar used to sweeten many drinks (as is grenadine). The ratio is traditionally one part water to two parts sugar, though you can play with the quantities to get the desired syrup.

Bring the sugar and water to a boil in a heavy saucepan and simmer for a few minutes, until the sugar dissolves. Cool and refrigerate.

YELLOWBIRD

SERVES 1

Yellow birds are like hummingbirds; if you offer them sugar, they'll gather. Offer a round of Yellow Birds to your friends, and they'll gather as well. You can find passion fruit syrup in Caribbean markets.

Freshly squeezed juice of 1 orange
Freshly squeezed juice of $1/2$ lemon
1 ounce Tia Maria
1 ounce dark rum
$1/4$ ounce passion fruit syrup
Orange slice, for garnish

Fill a Collins or rocks glass with ice. Add the orange juice, lemon juice, Tia Maria, rum, and syrup. Cover with a cocktail shaker and shake twice, or stir well six times. Garnish with the orange slice.

Recommended Listening

"Yellow Bird *(Tits Oiseau),*" by Harry Belafonte, from *Calypso Nights*

DAIQUIRI

SERVES 1

Though attributions abound, supposedly the daiquiri was dreamed up by an American mining engineer named Jennings Cox, who worked in the copper mines in the eastern Cuban village of Daiquiri in 1896. When some American friends were visiting, he ran out of gin and, afraid they wouldn't like the local hooch, dressed up the rum with limes and sugar. It was a hit, so he served the drink two years later to Americans who landed on the beach at Daiquiri during the Spanish-American War, and they in turn introduced their new drink, the daiquiri, back at the Army and Navy Club in Washington, D.C. This is one of those classic cocktails, now nearly lost to bad mixes and overly fruited renditions.

> **2 teaspoons powdered sugar**
> **Freshly squeezed juice of $^1/_2$ lime**
> **2 ounces Cuban-style or other golden rum**
> **$^1/_2$ ounce Cointreau (orange liqueur)**
> **Lime slice, for garnish**

Drop the sugar and lime juice into a rocks glass and mix with a spoon until a paste forms. Fill the glass with ice; add the rum and Cointreau. Cover with a cocktail shaker and shake vigorously for five seconds. Garnish with the lime slice.

Recommended Listening

"(You Gotta Walk and) Don't Look Back," by Peter Tosh and Mick Jagger, from *The Best of Peter Tosh*

HEMINGWAY DAIQUIRI

SERVES 1

Hemingway always requested a sugarless daiquiri loaded with rum ($2^1/2$ jiggers of Bacardi White Label per drink) at the Havana bar El Floridita. This version is tart and fresh.

Freshly squeezed juice of $^1/4$ lime

1 ounce freshly squeezed grapefruit juice (such as Texas Ruby Red grapefruit)

$^1/2$ ounce grenadine (see note)

$1^1/2$ ounces Bacardi white rum

Lime wedge, for garnish

Fill a mixing glass or shaker with ice. Add the lime juice, grapefruit juice, grenadine, and rum. Shake four times and strain into your favorite martini-style glass. Garnish with the lime wedge.

NOTE: *Grenadine is a syrup of pomegranate juice boiled with sugar. Use $^1/4$ ounce grenadine if you like your drink especially tart.*

Recommended Listening

"Los Blues," by Cuba Classics, from *Diablo al Infierno*

"[The] daiquiris had no taste of alcohol and felt, as you drank them, the way downhill glacier skiing feels running through powder snow and, after the sixth and eighth, felt like downhill glacier skiing feels when you are running unroped."
—Ernest Hemingway, from *Islands in the Stream*

LIMECAY

SERVES 2

This cocktail is a beautiful kiwi green, flecked with black seeds. Even if Lime Cay weren't a real island a few miles off the Jamaican coast, isn't it a great name?

3 ounces kiwi-lime base (see below)
1 ounce white rum
1^1/2 ounces sour mix (page 10)
2 lime slices, for garnish

Pour the kiwi-lime base, rum, and sour mix into a cocktail shaker filled with ice and shake well five times. Strain into two martini (or other fancy) glasses and garnish with the lime slices.

Recommended Listening

"Cool You," by Gregory Isaacs, from *Best of Volumes 1 & 2*

Kiwi-Lime Base

MAKES ABOUT 1 CUP

1 kiwifruit, peeled and roughly chopped
1 cup roughly chopped fresh pineapple
Freshly squeezed juice of 1 lime

Puree all ingredients in a blender or food processor until completely smooth and a little thick, about two to three minutes. Keep refrigerated in a covered container.

Best Caribbean Bars

Admiral's Inn, Antigua

Anse Chastenet Hotel, St. Lucia

Bananas, Vieques

Basil's Bar, Mustique

Blu Bar, Inn on the Blue Horizon, Vieques

Bomba's Shack, Tortola

Captain Tony's, Key West

Chicken Box, Nantucket*

Compleat Angler, Antigua

Cotton House, Mustique

Frangipani, Bequia

Hemingway's, Key West

Le Select, St. Bart's

Mad Dog, Virgin Gorda

Petit St. Vincent, Petit St. Vincent

Okay, Nantucket's a far cry from the West Indies, but the Chicken Box is a roadhouse that has been bringing blues and reggae to the faraway island for fifty years. A friend of mine was enjoying a bachelor party there when he spotted Jimmy Buffett at the bar. Buffett took to the tiny stage and played hits for a few hours with the house band. So set your sail for a long reach.

Basil's Bar, Mustique

KICK'EM JENNY

SERVES 1

Named after a submerged volcano off the north shore of Grenada—in 1902, sailors were shocked to see twenty-foot waves in the middle of the ocean, and to find that the water was bubbling hot—this is a good drink to shoot at the bar with friends. But it's not for the faint of heart.

> 1 tablespoon passion fruit syrup
> $1/4$ teaspoon vanilla syrup (see note)
> $1/2$ ounce gin
> 1 ounce Captain Morgan's Spiced Rum or other spiced rum
> 2 ounces Mount Gay Barbados Rum or other golden rum
> Club soda

Fill a Collins glass with ice. Add the syrups, gin, and rums and stir to mix. Top off with club soda. If shooting this drink, shake it over ice and strain it into shot glasses.

NOTE: *Use the kind of vanilla syrup that is used in coffees and sodas and is sold in Italian shops or coffee stores.*

Recommended Listening

"Hot Little Mama," by Johnny "Guitar" Wilson, from *Three Hours Past Midnight*

SOURCOCONUT

SERVES 1

Pucker up, baby. This exquisite drink is both coconutty and sour. Canned coconut milk can be found with the Asian products in supermarkets; don't confuse this with Coco López (cream of coconut).

>   2 ounces sour mix (page 10)
>   1 ounce coconut milk
>   1 ounce white rum
>   Lime slice, for garnish

Fill a rocks glass with ice. Add the sour mix, coconut milk, and rum and stir. Garnish with the lime slice.

Recommended Listening

"Coconut," by Harry Nilsson, from *Nilsson Schmilsson*

Shaken or Stirred

As a rule, shaking blends and aerates a drink, while stirring combines ingredients gently (which is preferable when you have a fizzy ingredient such as club soda).

BAHAMA MAMA

SERVES 1

One of my favorites, this foamy Bahama Mama has a hint of coconut. It comes to me courtesy of my friend Rip Gibson, who discovered it at a Miami bar. Coconut syrup can be found in specialty foods stores or gourmet-coffee shops.

$1^1/_2$ ounces Gosling's Bermuda Black Rum or other dark rum

$^1/_2$ ounce coconut syrup

$^1/_2$ ounce coffee-flavored brandy

4 ounces pineapple juice

Freshly squeezed juice of $^1/_2$ lemon

Fill a Collins glass with ice, add all the ingredients, and stir.

Recommended Listening

"Blow the Man Down (Flying Fish Sailor)", by Johnny Collins, from *Shanties and Songs of the Sea*

PLANTER'SPUNCH

SERVES 1

This heat-seeking missile, dating back to plantation days, will make you tingle. It's good on the porch late on a hot night.

2 ounces dark rum

1^1/2 ounces sour mix (page 10)

2 dashes angostura bitters

^{1}/2 teaspoon grenadine

Freshly squeezed juice of ^{1}/4 lime

Club soda

Orange slice and maraschino cherry, for garnish

Fill a rocks glass with ice. Add the rum, sour mix, bitters, grenadine, and lime juice, and stir. Top off with club soda, and garnish with the orange and cherry.

Recommended Listening

"The Lost Watch (Tik Tik Tik)," by Roaring Lion, from *Standing Proud*

"What harm in drinking can there be, since life and punch so well agree?"
—Thomas Blacklock, *Epigram on Punch*

RUMRUNNER

SERVES 1

During Prohibition, Captain William McCoy and other rumrunners brought rum, whiskey, and Champagne from the Bahamas and Europe to the "Rum Row" channel, twelve miles off the eastern seaboard, where it was sold in international waters. He never diluted his liquor, which became known as "the real McCoy."

> **2 teaspoons hot water**
> **2 teaspoons brown sugar**
> **Freshly squeezed juice of $1/2$ lime**
> **2 ounces Lemon Hart Demerara Rum**
> **4 dashes angostura bitters**
> **Lime wedge, for garnish**

In a rocks glass, add the water and sugar, and stir with a spoon until the sugar is almost completely dissolved. Fill the glass with ice; add the lime juice, rum, and bitters. Cover the glass with a cocktail shaker and shake three times. Garnish with the lime wedge.

Recommended Listening

"Will His Love Be Like His Rum," by Harry Belafonte, from *Best of Harry Belafonte*

WESTINDIANCOCKTAIL

SERVES 1

I remember sailing into a cove in the British Virgin Islands in a Hinckley South-wester 50 (it wasn't mine), swimming up to a bar that you could get to only by boat, and sipping a drink like this in my bathing suit. Just add music and the scent of frangipani.

> $3/4$ ounce banana liqueur (such as crème de banana)
> 1 ounce white rum
> 1 ounce sour mix (page 10)
> 2 ounces pineapple juice
> Pineapple wedge, for garnish

Fill a rocks or Collins glass with ice. Add the banana liqueur, rum, sour mix, and pineapple juice; cover with a mixing glass and shake five times. Garnish with the pineapple wedge.

Recommended Listening

"Montego Bay," by Bobby Bloom, from *The Best of Bobby Bloom;* or by Chet Atkins, from *Caribbean Guitar*

"The goddess made for me a cup of tea,
with a spot of rum;
But she herself drank only the rum,
without a spot of tea."

—Heinrich Heine

PIÑACOLADA

SERVES 2

One of the world's best-loved tropical drinks, the piña colada (Spanish for "strained pineapple") is a creamy concoction of coconut, pineapple, and rum. Stories abound about the history of this legendary blender drink; suffice it to say that it was invented in a San Juan hotel in the 1950s.

1 1/2 ounces Malibu Caribbean Rum or other coconut-flavored rum

1 ounce Coco López (cream of coconut)

3 ounces pineapple juice

2 cups ice

Freshly grated nutmeg

Combine all ingredients except nutmeg in a blender and give it hell for two to three minutes, or until smooth. (If the drink is not thick enough, add more ice; or for a rich, creamy drink, add 1 ounce of heavy whipping cream.) Pour into two festive glasses and dust the rims with nutmeg.

Recommended Listening

"Don't Worry, Be Happy," by Bobby McFerrin, from *Don't Worry, Be Happy*

SHAKENORSTIRRED

SERVES 1

This is a summery drink, with a smooth, soft fruitiness and delicate balance of flavors, laced lightly with raspberry and coconut. This vodka is also known as Stoli Razberi; if your bar's not stocked with it, it's worth getting for this recipe, because undoubtedly you'll find yourself using it for other summer drinks.

> 1 ounce Stolichnaya Raspberry Vodka
> 1 ounce Malibu Caribbean Rum or
>   other coconut-flavored rum
> 2 ounces sour mix (page 10)
> $^3/_4$ ounce cranberry juice cocktail
> $^3/_4$ ounce pineapple juice
> Pineapple wedge, for garnish

Pour vodka, rum, sour mix, cranberry juice, and pine-apple juice into either a mixing glass filled with ice or a Collins glass filled with ice. Shake the mixing glass four times and strain; or stir the mixture in the Collins glass. Garnish with the pineapple wedge.

Recommended Listening

"A Rum Tale," by Procol Harum, from *Grand Hotel*

BLUBARSUNSETRELAXER

SERVES 1

I'm a big fan of Vieques, a small island off the coast of Puerto Rico, where golf courses and tourism don't exist. With miles of pristine beaches and not a hot dog stand in sight, the island is what I suspect the West Indies might have felt like in the '30s. One of my favorite perches is at the cement Blu Bar at the Inn on the Blue Horizon, which overlooks a grassy plain reminiscent of an African savannah and, beyond, the ocean. After a hot day in the sun, relax at the bar, where you might be alone or sharing the stools with expats, bird lovers, and locals.

> 1 ounce light rum
> 1 ounce dark rum
> Splash of grenadine
> 2 ounces pineapple juice
> 2 ounces freshly squeezed orange juice

Fill a rocks glass with ice. Add the two rums and the grenadine. Fill with 2 ounces each of pineapple juice and orange juice. Top off with additional juice.

Recommended Listening

"Samba Pa Ti," by Santana, from *Abraxas*

2

TEQUILADRINKS

Made in Mexico from the fermented sap of the blue agave plant, tequila is a powerful tropical spirit that has enjoyed a renaissance of late, mostly thanks to the margarita's popularity. The spirit has ancient roots: long before sixteenth-century Spanish conquistadors built stills to produce tequila, natives made wine from the agave plant. Indeed, tequila was named after the town of Tequila in central Mexico, where the spirit is primarily produced. The name means "lava hill" in an indigenous Mexican language, because the agaves were grown there on a dormant volcano.

All tequila comes from several provinces in Mexico, primarily the Jalisco region. The king of Spain granted the first manufacturer's license to José Cuervo in 1758, and the spirit became so popular that twenty-five years later the king banned tequila because it threatened sales of Spanish wine and liqueurs. Eight years later, King Ferdinand IV realized that he could benefit more by taxation than from prohibition, and he lifted the tequila ban.

Like rum, tequila became increasingly popular during World War II, when other liquors were hard to procure. Its ascent was also fueled by Mexican movies in the '30s and '40s featuring tequila-drinking roughriders. By the '70s consumption declined, as tequila gained a reputation as an adolescent party drink. Tequila dusted off its reputation again in the '80s when the smooth **CHINACO,** the first premium tequila, was released in the United States. Today, tequila—riding the wave of interest in focused tastings of brews ranging from single malt scotches to varietal olive oils—is back in fashion.

Types of tequila include **WHITE, GOLD, REPOSADO,** and **AÑEJO. WHITE** (blanco) tequila, also called **PLATA** (silver) tequila, is a clear, fresh, unaged spirit. Robust and fiery, it's great on the rocks or in a cocktail. **GOLD** tequila is blanco tequila with caramel coloring and flavoring added to make it look aged.

REPOSADO (rested) tequila is aged in oak barrels from two to twelve months, which gives it a nuanced flavor and smoothness. It's delicious on the rocks or served neat. The finest variety is **AÑEJO** (aged) tequila. Aged for at least a year and up to four years, it's great sipped at room temperature in a snifter or on the rocks.

"Tequila has no history; there are no anecdotes confirming its birth.
This is how it's been since the beginning of time, for tequila is a gift from
the gods and they don't tend to offer fables when bestowing favors.
That is the job of mortals, the children of panic and tradition."

—Mexican poet Alvaro Mutis

GREENAGAVE

SERVES 1

The flavor of tangy melon liqueur blended with tart lime and tequila will make you hungry for hot peppers.

> 1 ounce Midori or other melon liqueur (see note)
> 1 ounce Chinaco Blanco
> Freshly squeezed juice of $1/2$ lime
> Lime slice, for garnish

Fill a cocktail shaker with ice. Pour the Midori, tequila, and lime juice over the ice. Shake vigorously for 15 seconds, then strain into a martini glass. Garnish with the lime slice.

NOTE: *Midori is a bright green (it looks great on the beach) honeydew melon–flavored liqueur from Japan that was introduced to the world at Studio 54 in 1978 (the year the Bee Gees were staying alive).*

Recommended Listening

"Pour Me Another Tequila," by Eddie Rabbitt, from *All-Time Greatest Hits*

TORTUGA

SERVES 1

This drink is a little limy, a little sweet. Blue curaçao is a liqueur made from the peel of bitter Curaçao oranges, which were originally only grown on the island of Curaçao. By the way, blue curaçao is identical to orange curaçao in flavor; only the color differs.

> **3 cubes brown sugar, or 3 teaspoons brown sugar**
> **1 tablespoon hot water**
> **1^1/2 ounces tequila**
> **Freshly squeezed juice of ^{1}/2 lime**
> **1 teaspoon blue curaçao**
> **Lime slice, for garnish**

Place the sugar cubes and hot water in a tall mixing glass, allowing water to dissolve the sugar (it does not have to be completely dissolved, just no longer a cube). Add ice to fill the mixing glass then the tequila, lime juice, and curaçao; shake six times. Strain the mixture into any cocktail glass. Garnish with the lime slice.

Recommended Listening

"Sugaree," by Gregory Isaacs, from *Fire on the Mountain II*
(Reggae Celebrates the Grateful Dead)

MYBLUEHEAVEN

SERVES 1

A blue margarita of sorts, this drink is smooth and slightly tangy with lime. Use kosher salt instead of margarita salt—it's essentially the same, but less expensive. (Or, you can use regular salt, which is finer and has twice the salt grain for the same measure as kosher salt.) Dusting with salt and sugar offers a nice salty-sweet tension that complements the tequila and lime.

$1/4$ **ounce freshly squeezed lime juice, plus 1 lime wedge for garnish**

Approximately 1 tablespoon kosher salt and 1 tablespoon sugar, mixed, for glass rim

1 ounce tequila

$1/2$ **ounce Cointreau**

2 ounces sour mix (page 10)

1 teaspoon blue curaçao

Run the lime wedge around the rim of a margarita or martini glass to moisten slightly and place salt and sugar mixture on a small plate. Turn the glass over and dip into the mixture. Fill a cocktail shaker with ice; add the tequila, Cointreau, sour mix, lime juice, and curaçao; shake vigorously ten to fifteen times. Strain the contents of the shaker into the glass. Garnish with the lime wedge.

NOTE: *You can serve this drink straight up or on the rocks, whatever floats your boat.*

Recommended Listening

"My Blue Heaven," by Glenn Miller, from *Forever Gold*

MARGARITA

SERVES 1

Although legends abound of this drink's origin, it likely was invented by a Tijuana restaurateur in 1938, who mixed it up for a local actress. The margarita became the #1 cocktail in the United States.

1 tablespoon kosher salt

Lime wedge, plus $1/2$ lime (if it's not a juicy lime, use a whole lime, cut in half)

2 ounces El Tesoro Añejo Tequila or other high-quality gold tequila

$1^3/4$ ounces Grand Marnier

Lime slice, for garnish

Place the salt on a small plate. Rub the rim of a martini, champagne, or margarita glass with the lime wedge, then dip it in the salt to coat the rim. Set aside.

Fill a mixing glass or cocktail shaker with ice; add tequila and Grand Marnier. Squeeze the lime half into the container and drop in the rind. Shake six times and strain quickly into the drinking glass. Garnish with the lime slice.

Recommended Listening

"Margaritaville," by Jimmy Buffett, from *Changes in Latitudes, Changes in Attitudes*

BLUMARGARITA

SERVES 1

Even jaded drinkers will take notice of the aqua color of this drink from Blu Bar at the Inn on the Blue Horizon—it looks like something you want to dive into.

> 1 tablespoon kosher salt
>
> Lime wedge
>
> 1³/4 ounces Herradura Silver Natural Tequila or other premium white or gold tequila
>
> 1/4 ounce blue curaçao
>
> 6 ounces sour mix (page 10)

Place the salt on a small plate. Rub the rim of a margarita-style glass with the lime wedge, then dip it in the salt to coat the rim. Set aside.

Pour the tequila and curaçao into an ice-filled shaker. Add the sour mix, shake, and pour into the prepared glass.

Recommended Listening

"I Can See Clearly Now," by Johnny Nash, from *I Can See Clearly Now*

> "Wasted away again in Margaritaville
> Searchin' for my lost shaker of salt
> Some people claim that there's a woman to blame
> But I know, it's my own damn fault."
>
> —Jimmy Buffett

TEQUILASUNRISE

SERVES 1

Smooth, tropical, and peachy—enough of these and you may see Michelle Pfeiffer or Kurt Russell in your dreams. The schnapps gives this classic drink a slight twist.

> 1 ounce tequila
> 1 ounce peach schnapps
> $2^1/_2$ ounces freshly squeezed orange juice
> 1 teaspoon grenadine
> Maraschino cherry, lime wedge, or orange wedge for garnish (optional)

Fill a cocktail shaker or mixing glass with ice. Add the tequila, schnapps, and orange juice and shake ten times. Pour grenadine into a martini glass, so it sits on the bottom. Strain the drink mixture into the glass. Add the garnish.

Recommended Listening

"Tropical Merengue," by Percy Faith, from *Greatest Hits*

CARIBBEANCOWBOY

SERVES 1

This drink offers a full palate of flavors, with its wild combinations and the jolt from the tequila. You can find guava juice in Mexican or Caribbean markets.

1 1/2 ounces Chinaco Blanco or other high-quality white tequila
2 ounces guava juice
1 ounce Cointreau
1 ounce sour mix (page 10)
1 teaspoon grenadine
Lime slice, for garnish

Fill a mixing glass with ice. Add the tequila, guava juice, Cointreau, sour mix, and grenadine; shake four times and strain into a stylish martini-style glass. Garnish with the lime slice.

Recommended Listening

"I Think I'll Just Stay Here and Drink," by Merle Haggard & the Strangers, from *Western Swing, Various Artists*

One of the few female pirates of the early eighteenth century, Anne Bonny was a rich Irish girl whose father had high expectations for her. When she hooked up with a sailor ("not worth a Groat," according to a 1724 book), her father turned her out. So Anne's husband, disappointed that her financial prospects weren't nearly so bonny, dressed her as a man and took to the high seas with her. Whenever she got pregnant, he'd plunk her down on the beaches of Cuba, and pick her up again after she'd delivered.

HONEYSUCKLE

SERVES 1

Interesting drinks have a beginning, middle, and end. You'll find them all in this drink, from the initial subtle floral flavor to the coconut middle and the citrusy finish.

1 ounce tequila

$^1/_2$ ounce peach schnapps

$^1/_2$ ounce Malibu Caribbean Rum or other coconut-flavored rum

2 ounces pineapple juice

1 ounce cranberry juice

Lime slice, for garnish

Fill a mixing glass with ice; add the tequila, schnapps, rum, and fruit juices. Shake four times and strain into a martini-style glass. Garnish with the lime slice.

Recommended Listening

"Sweet and Dandy," by Toots and the Maytals, from the soundtrack of *The Harder They Come*

GINGERITA

SERVES 2

Smooth and lush, Gingerita has a spicy aftertaste. Ginger cordial can be found at specialty food stores such as Dean & DeLuca.

> **2 ounces tequila**
> **$1/2$ ounce Triple Sec**
> **1 ounce sour mix (page 10)**
> **$1/4$ ounce ginger cordial (see note)**
> **Freshly squeezed juice of $1/4$ lime**
> **1 ounce Coco López (cream of coconut)**
> **$2^1/2$ cups ice**

Place all ingredients in a blender and whir until smooth, about two to three minutes. Fill two short glasses.

NOTE: *I use the Belvoir brand of ginger cordial, which can be found at Dean & Deluca. It's made with fresh gingerroot, so use it sparingly.*

Recommended Listening

"Tiney Winey," by Byron Lee and the Dragonaires, from *Soca Tremor*

BELIZE

SERVES 1

Light on the tequila, this balanced drink is fruity but not overly sweet. I prefer to use 100 percent cranberry juice, but a blend also works.

1 ounce white tequila

3 ounces pineapple juice

**1 ounce cranberry juice
  or cranberry juice cocktail**

1 ounce sour mix (page 10)

$^1/_2$ ounce grenadine

Fill a rocks glass with ice. Add all ingredients; cover and shake five times.

Recommended Listening

"Come Sail Away," by Styx, from *Return to Paradise*

OTHERSPIRITS

Granted, when I land in the islands, the first drink I request is always some sort of rum cocktail (which gets your blood moving in the tropical heat). But while I never tire of a cocktail whose driving force is Kill Devil, there are other spirits that help create a damn good drink.

Angostura bitters, for example, was invented in the Caribbean littoral by a Venezuelan surgeon in General Simón Bolívar's army as a tonic for tropical jungle stomach disorders. The patients and passing ship crews raved so much about the herbal tonic that the doctor abandoned his practice to produce the bitters, which he which he named after the town that was Bolívar's headquarters. When the revolution heated up, the doctor and his family moved to Trinidad, where angostura bitters has been produced ever since.

It came to be revered as a flavor enhancer for food and drink as well as a cure-all for stomach ailments. These days, angostura bitters is underused and underappreciated—which is a pity, since it can turn a good drink into a great cocktail, with the perfect astringent pull and a beautiful pink color. This chapter offers examples of how Caribbean flavors other than rum can be combined to bring the taste of the tropics to your bar.

STICKYWICKET

SERVES 1

I can't get enough of these thirst-quenching drinks, either in the islands or up north. Angostura bitters is a secret ingredient in many bartenders' drinks that adds a lovely astringent quality.

> 1 teaspoon granulated sugar
> 4 dashes angostura bitters
> 2 ounces gin
> $1/2$ lemon, freshly squeezed
> 2 ounces club soda
> Cucumber slice, for garnish

Fill a rocks glass with ice. Add the sugar, bitters, and gin. Squeeze in the lemon juice, then drop the rind into the glass. Cover and shake well to dissolve the sugar, then top with club soda. Garnish with the cucumber slice.

Recommended Listening

"Joshua Gone Barbados," by Tom Rush, from *The Very Best of Tom Rush: No Regrets*

BETWEENTHESHEETS

SERVES 1

This drink will make you stand up at attention. Though heavy on the liquor, its flavor is well rounded, with a velvety aftertaste.

> **Freshly squeezed juice of $1/2$ lemon**
> **$3/4$ ounce Triple Sec**
> **$3/4$ ounce brandy**
> **$3/4$ ounce white rum**
> **1 ounce sour mix (page 10)**
> **Lime slice, for garnish**

Fill a mixing glass with ice; add the lemon juice, Triple Sec, brandy, rum, and sour mix. Shake five times and strain into a martini-style glass. Garnish with the lime slice.

Recommended Listening

"No Hurry, No Problem," by Brannan Lane, from *Caribbean Dream*

YANKEE CLIPPER

SERVES 1

Slightly tart, the Yankee Clipper is cool, light, and refreshing. Many Caribbean drinks have a rounded softness from tropical fruits, but cranberry and citrus juices make this drink more bracing.

> 2 ounces vodka
>
> 2 ounces cranberry juice (not cranberry juice cocktail)
>
> 1 teaspoon passion fruit syrup
>
> 2 ounces freshly squeezed grapefruit juice (preferably Texas Ruby Red)
>
> 1 ounce sour mix (page 10)
>
> Lime wedge, for garnish

Fill a Collins glass with ice. Pour in the vodka, cranberry juice, passion fruit syrup, grapefruit juice, and sour mix and stir. Garnish with the lime wedge.

Recommended Listening

"Vahevala (Home of Sailors)," by Loggins & Messina, from *Sittin' In*

PINKDRINK

SERVES 2

Metal cocktail shakers are handy for gauging a drink's readiness: when a frost appears on the shaker (after approximately fifteen seconds), your drink is well chilled.

> **3 ounces watermelon purée (see note)**
> **Freshly squeezed juice of $1/2$ lime**
> **1 ounce vodka**
> **1 ounce Cointreau**
> **1 ounce pineapple juice**
> **2 orange slices, for garnish**

Fill a cocktail shaker with ice. Add the watermelon purée, lime juice, vodka, Cointreau, and pineapple juice and shake three or four times to blend. Strain into martini or other pretty glasses, and garnish with the orange slices.

NOTE: *To purée watermelon, put 1 cup of seeded watermelon in a food processor or blender and run until smooth, about two to three minutes.*

Recommended Listening

"No Woman, No Cry" by Bob Marley and the Wailers, from *Exodus*

MARTINIQUE

SERVES 1

This tart, fruity little French cocktail is named after an island settled by the French in 1635. Martinique was also the birthplace of Napoléon's Josephine, who was crowned empress of France in 1804.

> $^1/_2$ ounce crème de cassis (black currant–flavored liqueur)
> $^1/_2$ ounce peach schnapps
> 2 ounces cranberry juice cocktail
> 2 ounces freshly squeezed orange juice
> Freshly squeezed juice of $^1/_4$ lemon

Fill a Collins glass with ice. Add all the ingredients and stir. Voilà!

Recommended Listening

"Reggae Calypso," by Yellowman, from *King Yellowman*

JAMAIC'NMECRAZY

SERVES 1

This vodka punch should always be made with fresh sour mix, which is easy to prepare (see page 10). If you keep a pitcher of the mix handy in your refrigerator, you'll find yourself reaching for it often.

> 1¹/2 ounces Stolichnaya Orange Vodka

1¹/2 ounces Stolichnaya Orange Vodka

1 ounce sour mix (page 10)

2 ounces freshly squeezed orange juice

1 ounce pineapple juice

1/2 ounce Triple Sec

1 teaspoon grenadine

Fill a rocks glass with ice. Add all the ingredients; cover and shake until foamy (about five shakes).

Recommended Listening

"Here I Come!" by Dennis Brown, from *Some Like It Hot*

Jamaican Patois

Bedrin, wa gwaan?	What's up, man?
How yuh bite up so today?	Why are you in such a mood?
Duh stew's comin' up.	The stew's cooking.
No badda bawl im soon come back.	Don't bother crying, he'll soon be back.
An yuh swallow dat?	And you believe that?
Me bleach hard lass night.	I partied hard last night.
Coo pon dat bwoy!	Look at that boy!

Yu haffi learn evry-*ting!*

BERMUDATRIANGLE

SERVES 1

My friend Nancy Thomas taught me a thing or two about Lillet (pronounced *lih-LAY*), a lovely French apéritif that lends a clean botanical element to drinks and serves as a handy "spacer" if a drink is too strong and needs to be "opened up." (*Apéritif* comes from the Latin word *aperire*, "to open.") Lillet Blanc, which James Bond always preferred in his Martinis, is modestly alcoholic, made with wine, liqueurs, fruits, and herbs.

> **2 ounces Lillet Blanc**
> **1^1/$_2$ ounces amaretto**
> **Freshly squeezed juice of 1 lime**
> **Up to 1 ounce club soda (optional)**
> **Lime wedge, for garnish**

Fill a rocks glass with ice. Pour the Lillet, amaretto, and lime juice over the ice. Place a stainless steel mixing cup over the glass and shake five times. Remove the mixing vessel, stir in the club soda, and garnish with the lime wedge.

Recommended Listening

"Bermuda Triangle," by Fleetwood Mac, from *Heroes Are Hard to Find*

HIBISCUSCOSMOPOLITAN

SERVES 1

Bold as red lipstick on a dame, sorrel is an edible hibiscus that blooms in the islands in December. (Don't confuse it with the European herb of the same name.) The sepals are steeped to make a tea that's as popular in Jamaica as iced tea is in the South. You'll find sorrel at West Indian markets, and it's well worth the effort. (And the tartlike scarlet color is gorgeous.)

1 ounce sorrel tea (see opposite)
$^1/_2$ ounce Triple Sec
$^1/_2$ ounce Rose's Lime Juice
1 ounce vodka
$^1/_2$ ounce sour mix (page 10)
Lime slice, for garnish

Fill a cocktail shaker with ice and add the sorrel tea, Triple Sec, Rose's, vodka, and sour mix. Shake four times and strain into a martini-style glass. Garnish with the lime slice.

Recommended Listening

"Hot Hot Hot," by Buster Poindexter, from *Hot Hot Hot*

STIRITUP

SERVES 1

This beautiful scarlet drink is refreshing and tart. To make a sangría-like drink, mix up a batch in a punch bowl and add fresh fruit.

> 1 ounce sour mix (page 10)
> 4 ounces sorrel tea (see below)
> $3/4$ ounce amaretto
> Splash of club soda
> 2 orange slices, for garnish

Fill a Collins glass with ice. Add the sour mix, sorrel tea, and amaretto, then top off with a splash of club soda. Stir it up with a straw or festive stirrer, and garnish with the orange slices.

Recommended Listening

"Stir It Up," by Bob Marley and the Wailers, from *Catch a Fire*

Sorrel Tea

To make sorrel tea, immerse 1 cup of dried flowers in 2 quarts of boiling water in a large nonreactive pot and steep for at least one hour and up to one day. (You can also steep the flowers with some grated fresh ginger—1 tablespoon of ginger to 1 cup of sorrel flowers.)

To serve as iced tea, add sugar to taste. Or, for a traditional Caribbean Christmas drink, add sugar and rum and serve over ice with a twist of lime.

BLUETOPAZ

SERVES 1

This light cocktail is good before dinner, or served with spicy foods. Lillet is a delightful old-fashioned French apéritif (page 63) that, if your grandmother hasn't already turned you on to it, is well worth discovering.

> $1/2$ ounce blue curaçao
> 2 ounces Lillet Blanc
> 2 ounces sour mix (page 10)

Fill a cocktail shaker with ice; add all the ingredients. Shake to chill, then strain into a pretty glass.

Recommended Listening

"A Sailboat in the Moonlight" by Billie Holiday, from *Love Me or Leave Me*

HEATWAVE

SERVES 1

This drink is sour, zippy, and not too sweet. Always freshly squeeze your lime juice; it makes a difference in the success of a cocktail.

1 ounce gin
$^1/_2$ ounce Campari
3 ounces pineapple juice
$^1/_4$ ounce freshly squeezed lime juice

Fill a cocktail shaker with ice; add all the ingredients. Shake ten times, then strain into a martini-style glass or a small tumbler.

Recommended Listening

"Heat Wave," by Linda Rondstadt,
from *Prisoner in Disguise*

GREENFROG

SERVES 1

There's nothing like a light, fruity drink that's well spaced, yielding the "cresting" effect of a great cocktail.

$^1/_2$ **ounce blue curaçao**
$1^1/_2$ **ounces vodka**
4 ounces pineapple juice
7-Up, to taste

Fill a rocks glass with ice and add the ingredients in order.

Recommended Listening

"Coconut Island," by Junior Brown, from *Twelve Shades of Brown*

Going Tropo

- Toss your wristwatch and alarm clock into a drawer.
- Eat fresh, eat local.
- Enjoy plenty of music and rum.
- Absolutely no personal organizers, cell phones, or laptops.
- Stay where the inside and outside are the same.
- Swim under a full moon.
- Boogie-board or bodysurf.
- Fall asleep in a hammock under a sea grape tree.
- Lose yourself in the kind of novel you wouldn't read at home.
- Snorkel for sand dollars to decorate your Christmas tree.
- Wear white cotton.
- Say the sun did it.

COCOLOCO

SERVES 1

This frothy drink, with its nutty creaminess, is soothing on a steamy night.

> 1 ounce Kahlúa
> $^1/_2$ ounce banana liqueur (such as crème de banana)
> 4 ounces milk
> 1 teaspoon Coco López (cream of coconut)

Fill a rocks glass with ice, add all the ingredients, top with a cocktail shaker, and shake vigorously ten times.

Recommended Listening

"Coconut Boogaloo," by Medeski, Martin, and Wood, from *Combustication*

FLYINGBOAT

SERVES 1

Delivering boats to the British Virgins, I spent many evenings on deck, checking out the stars and listening to the Elvis of the Islands. This son of a son of a sailor (his grandfather skippered a five-masted barentine that ferried lumber from New Orleans to the Caribbean) has his own Flying Boat—a Grumman seaplane that he has taken to the islands and lived to write about it. If you still haven't cottoned on to the person I'm talking about, send me a coconut telegraph.

$1^1/_2$ ounces Southern Comfort
$^1/_2$ ounce amaretto
2 ounces pineapple juice
1 ounce cranberry juice cocktail
1 teaspoon grenadine

Fill a rocks glass with ice, add all the ingredients, cover, and shake once to blend. Serve on the rocks (perish the thought).

VARIATION: *Strain this mixture, fill a lot of shot glasses with it, and serve a round.*

Recommended Listening

"Caribbean Queen," by Billy Ocean, from *Suddenly*

NONALCOHOLIC DRINKS

Mama said there'd be days like this. Days when you're feeling hot hot hot and walking on sunshine and just want to dive into Margaritaville or go for that boat drink that gets your mojo working and makes Tiney Winey want to rumba—days that prompt you, in the words of a sailing buddy, to tack hard against the wind and send someone out on a harness to judge that, indeed, the sun *has* gone below the yardarm, if only for a second. Then there are days when girls just want to have fun, without rum, but don't want to be relegated to a prim Shirley Temple with a bright red cherry. Days when your rum runner has sprung a leak, or you're on the wagon, or on a long reach, or looking for the Mai without the Tai. Days that you want the zing without the zinger. What really sets Caribbean cocktails apart is the nonalcoholic ingredients, such as fresh ginger, tropical fruits, and coconut; take out the hooch and you still have a great drink. So put the lime in the coconut and drink it all up.

MANGOMOON

SERVES 2 TO 4

With sweet, smooth mango spiced with ginger, this is an adult cocktail without the booze. Mango drink can be found in West Indian markets in cardboard juice boxes, similar to the boxes soymilk is sold in.

> 12 ounces mango drink
> 1 ounce ginger cordial (see page 52)
> 4 ounces sour mix (page 10)

In a small pitcher, add all the ingredients and stir three or four times. Fill four small glasses or two large glasses with ice and pour in the mixture.

Recommended Listening

"Island in the West Indies," by Lena Horne, from *Lena Goes Latin*

KIWIPRESSÉ

SERVES 1

Good with spicy foods, this dame is a gorgeous kiwi green, so let her shine in a fancy glass.

> **2 parts kiwi-lime base (page 29)**
> **1 part ginger ale**
> **Lime slice, for garnish**

Choose your glass size and fill halfway with crushed ice (or regular ice will do). Fill the glass two-thirds full with kiwi-lime base and top with ginger ale. Garnish with the lime slice.

Recommended Listening

"Sail Away," by David Gray, from *White Ladder*

SLIPPERYBANANA

SERVES 2

Add a spoonful of wheat germ to the blender if you want to go to heaven. This smoothie is creamy, but not overly sweet. To make the ice cubes, fill four molds of an ice cube tray with orange juice and two molds with pineapple juice. Chill in the freezer until frozen solid, several hours or overnight.

ICE CUBES
2 to 3 tablespoons freshly squeezed orange juice
2 to 3 tablespoons pineapple juice

DRINKS
1 frozen banana
1 cup coconut milk
1 ounce pineapple juice
1 ounce freshly squeezed orange juice

To make the drinks, place the banana, coconut milk, pineapple juice, and orange juice in a blender and process until smooth. Add frozen juice cubes and blend until smooth. Pour into two glasses, dividing equally. Garnish with the pineapple wedges and serve immediately.

Recommended Listening

"Day-O (Banana Boat Song)", by Harry Belafonte, from *Calypso*

JENNY

SERVES 1

My husband, Joe, created this perfect non-alcoholic cocktail for me. Angostura gives the drink a pink blush.

> **1 cup tonic water**
> **3 to 4 dashes angostura bitters**
> **Lime wedge**

Fill a rocks or Collins glass with ice. Add the tonic and bitters; squeeze in the lime juice, then drop in the rind. Stir and serve.

Recommended Listening

"Jump in the Line," by Harry Belafonte, from *Harry Belafonte's Greatest Hits Collection*

The fairest land ever eyes beheld. The mountains touch the sky.
—Columbus, about Jamaica

It is the most beautiful thing I have ever seen. My eyes never tire to see such a greenery.
—Columbus, about Martinique

I have never seen a more beautiful place . . . such marvelous beauty that it surpasses all others.
—Columbus, about Cuba

Do you think he was going in circles?

MANGO**MORNING**

SERVES 3

With its creamy mango taste, this feels like drinking a Caribbean morning. The Looza brand of passion fruit nectar can be found at most supermarkets.

1 cup passion fruit syrup

2 ripe mangoes, peeled, pitted, and coarsely chopped

8 ice cubes

$^1/_2$ cup whole-milk yogurt

In a blender, process all the ingredients until smooth. Pour into three glasses and serve immediately, while still cold.

Recommended Listening

"The Mango Song," by Phish, from *Picture of Nectar*

CITRUSSWING

SERVES 2

Thick and creamy, this lemony drink is great on a hot day. To make the ice cubes, fill four molds of an ice cube tray with orange juice and two molds with lime juice. Chill in the freezer until frozen solid, several hours or overnight.

ICE CUBES

2 to 3 tablespoons freshly squeezed
   orange juice

2 to 3 tablespoons freshly squeezed lime juice

DRINKS

1 cup lemon sorbet

5 ice cubes

$1^{1}/_{2}$ teaspoons grated fresh ginger

$^{1}/_{2}$ tablespoon honey

$^{1}/_{2}$ cup pineapple juice

2 lime wedges, for garnish

To make the drinks, place the sorbet, plain ice cubes, orange juice cubes, lime juice cubes, ginger, honey, and pineapple juice in a blender and process until smooth.
Pour into two glasses, dividing equally. Garnish with the lime wedges and serve immediately.

Recommended Listening

"Sloop John B," by the Beach Boys, from *Pet Sounds*

VIRGINVOODOO

SERVES 2

This smoothie can be gussied up with rum, but it's also awfully good by itself. It's delicious garnished with a bit of freshly grated nutmeg.

$^1/_2$ cup whole-milk yogurt

1 cup pineapple juice

2 teaspoons vanilla extract

2 frozen bananas

Pinch of freshly grated nutmeg (optional), for garnish

In a blender, process the yogurt, pineapple juice, vanilla extract, and bananas until smooth. Pour into two glasses, dividing equally. Garnish with nutmeg.

Recommended Listening

"Message in a Bottle," by The Police, from *Regatta de Blanc*

SNACKSAND APPETIZERS

Colonists and African slaves from the 1500s on had an extraordinary culinary impact on the islands. Spaniards introduced rice, beans, lemons, limes, coconuts, figs, date palms, and ginger to the Caribbean. West Africans brought yams, plantains, okra, and pigeon peas, as well as knowledge about preserving and spicing foods. The English added curries to the mix (lamb was hard to find, so they substituted goat), along with turmeric, black pepper, Christmas puddings, and Easter buns. After the emancipation of slaves in the nineteenth century, planters imported workers from China (who introduced stir-fry techniques to Trinidad) and indentured servants from India (who brought star fruit, tamarind, mangoes, and cayenne). To this day you'll find curries in Trinidad, *asopao* in Puerto Rico, and *bébelé aux fruits de mer* in Martinique.

Pre-1500 native influences are not as broadly prevalent—the original inhabitants are all but extinct in the Caribbean, with the exception of Dominica—but in Jamaica the Arawaks left a profound mark on the culinary world when they teamed up with escaped African slaves and invented jerk cooking. Other native ways are evident in the traditions of cooking with the indigenous fruits, vegetables, and fish of the islands.

COD CAKES WITH CURRIED BERMUDA ONION RELISH

SERVES 8 AS APPETIZERS OR MAKES 16 TO 20 HORS D'OEUVRE BITES

The sweet, slightly curried relish provides an unusual flavor contrast to the fried cakes in this Bermudan dish. You'll find salt cod in the seafood section of supermarkets, and panko (fluffy Japanese bread crumbs) in Asian markets or gourmet stores. You can make the cod cake mixture up to twenty-four hours ahead and store it in the refrigerator. Before you make the cod cakes, you'll need to soak the cod in cold water for 24 hours, changing the water at least once.

ONION RELISH

- 2 tablespoons vegetable oil or olive oil
- 2 large Bermuda or red onions, thinly sliced
- $1^1/2$ teaspoons curry powder
- 5 teaspoons malt or white vinegar
- 2 teaspoons sugar
- $1/2$ teaspoon salt

COD CAKES

- 1 pound salt cod
- 3 whole cloves garlic, unpeeled
- 1 teaspoon olive oil
- 2 medium russet potatoes, peeled and chopped into small dice
- $1/2$ red bell pepper, finely chopped
- 2 tablespoons finely chopped fresh parsley
- 2 tablespoons mayonnaise
- 1 tablespoon Dijon mustard
- Salt and pepper
- 1 egg
- 2 tablespoons water
- $1/2$ cup flour
- 2 cups seasoned bread crumbs or panko
- Vegetable oil, for frying

To make the onion relish, heat the oil in a sauté pan over medium-high heat. Add the onions and curry powder and cook until the onions are soft, approximately 10 minutes. Add the vinegar, sugar, and salt and continue cooking until the onions have a deep golden color, approximately 15 minutes or longer.

Preheat the oven to 350°F. Coat the garlic in olive oil, wrap in foil, and roast for 15 to 20 minutes. Remove from the oven and let cool. When cool, cut the cloves open and squeeze out the soft roasted garlic.

Place the cod in a fresh pot of water. Bring to a boil, reduce heat, and simmer for 8 minutes. Drain, cool, and chop the cod. In a large pot of boiling salted water, cook the potatoes until soft, about 10 minutes. Cool slightly. In a large mixing bowl, combine the cod, potatoes, roasted garlic, bell pepper, parsley, mayonnaise, mustard, salt, and pepper. Mix well. Form the mixture into 8 large cakes or 16 to 20 bite-size cakes.

Make an egg wash by beating 1 egg with 2 tablespoons of water till well mixed. Place the flour, egg wash, and breadcrumbs in 3 separate shallow bowls. Coat the cakes in flour, then egg wash, and finally bread crumbs.

Heat 3 tablespoons of vegetable oil in a sauté pan over medium heat and cook the cakes in batches until brown all over, approximately 5 minutes per side for large cakes and 3 minutes for smaller ones. Transfer to paper towels to drain. Repeat the procedure, adding more oil as needed, until all the cakes are cooked. Serve immediately, with warm onion relish.

GRILLED SHRIMP WITH CARIBBEAN SPICE PASTE

MAKES 12

With the curry, garlic, ginger, and lime, this spice paste is a typically Caribbean taste. If you're in a hurry, you can cheat and substitute Jump Up and Kiss Me Original Hot Sauce with Passion for the paste.

 4 teaspoons curry powder
 2 teaspoons ground cumin
 2 small cloves garlic, or 1 large clove
 2 teaspoons finely chopped fresh ginger
 2 green onions, white and pale green parts only, chopped
 3 tablespoons freshly squeezed lime juice
 2 teaspoons sugar
 1 teaspoon salt
 3 tablespoons olive oil
 12 jumbo shrimp, unpeeled

Combine the curry powder, cumin, garlic, ginger, green onions, lime juice, sugar, and salt in a blender or food processor and blend on high. With the motor running, add the oil in a slow drizzle to form a paste. Set aside. (This paste will keep for up to two days, covered and refrigerated.)

Using scissors, cut the raw shrimp down the back through the shell, and remove the vein. Using your fingers, gently loosen the shell from the flesh, keeping it attached. Gently pull open the shell of each shrimp and push some of the paste over the back of the shrimp under the shell. Close the shells around the shrimp. Cover with plastic wrap and refrigerate at least $1/2$ hour and up to 5 hours. Let the shrimp come up to room temperature before cooking, approximately 15 minutes.

Preheat a grill to medium-high. Grill the shrimp until the shells are charred on one side, about 3 minutes. Turn and cook for another 2 minutes, or just until the shrimp are opaque throughout. Serve hot.

JAMAICAN PATTIES

MAKES 24 PATTIES

Although meat patties originated in Haiti, they've become a Jamaican treasure, with a curry flavor that reflects the British colonial influence there. In the islands, people eat meat patties for lunch, dinner, or snacks, or with beer at a bar. Easy to make, they are an attention-grabbing appetizer, with a kaleidoscope of flavors from the lamb, curry, sweet potatoes, jalapeños, and lime. Serve these patties during cocktails, or with a carrot-ginger soup for lunch. The prep is easy; put them together in the morning and refrigerate them until you're ready to bake. If you want to add spice to the night, don't seed the jalapeños. Serve with hot sauce for dipping.

PASTRY

2 tablespoons black or brown mustard seeds

$1^1/2$ cups flour

1 tablespoon curry powder

1 teaspoon ground cumin

$1/2$ teaspoon salt

$1/2$ cup (1 stick) chilled butter, chopped

$1/3$ cup ice water

1 tablespoon malt vinegar

1 egg yolk, beaten

FILLING

1 tablespoon canola oil

$1/2$ medium onion, diced

$1/2$ jalapeño chile, seeded and minced

$1/2$ teaspoon minced fresh ginger

1 plum tomato, seeded and diced

$1/2$ sweet potato, peeled and cut into medium dice

4 ounces lamb, diced

Salt and pepper

1 tablespoon freshly squeezed lime juice

1 cup roasted chopped unsalted cashews

$1/2$ cup flour, for dusting

1 egg beaten with 1 tablespoon water, for egg wash

Hot sauce

To make the pastry, scatter the mustard seeds in a small skillet over medium heat. Shake or stir occasionally and cook until the seeds are fragrant, about 2 to 3 minutes. Combine the flour, curry, cumin, salt, and toasted seeds in a food processor and pulse once to combine. Add the butter and process until the mixture resembles fine crumbs.

In another bowl, combine the ice water, vinegar, and egg yolk. Add the wet mixture to the processor and pulse until a ball forms. Cover the dough in plastic wrap and refrigerate for 45 minutes. (The dough may be kept in the refrigerator for several days; it should be brought up to room temperature before rolling out.)

Preheat the oven to 350°F. To make the filling, heat the canola oil in a sauté pan over medium heat. Add the onion, chile, ginger, tomato, and sweet potato. Cook until the onion and sweet potato begin to soften, about 8 minutes. Add the lamb and continue to cook, stirring occasionally, for approximately 5 minutes or until the lamb is cooked. Season with salt and pepper. Allow the mixture to cool, then add the lime juice and cashews.

Roll out the dough on a surface lightly dusted with the remaining $1/2$ cup flour to $1/8$-inch thickness. Using a 3-inch round cutter, cut the dough into circles. Place 1 tablespoon of filling onto half of each dough round. Brush the edges with the egg wash. Fold the dough over the filling to make a semicircle and press the edges to seal. Brush the top with more egg wash. Place the patties on a parchment-paper-lined baking sheet or a baking sheet sprayed with non-stick vegetable oil spray and bake in the oven for 10 minutes. Serve immediately with hot sauce.

VARIATION: *You can substitute ground beef for the lamb.*

JERK PORK AND PINEAPPLE SKEWERS

MAKES 10 SKEWERS

Jerk is an ancient Jamaican method of cooking well-spiced meat slowly over a pimento-wood fire. Jerk huts dot the sides of roads in Jamaica, serving wondrously complex jerk.

1 bunch green onions, white and pale green parts only

1 tablespoon minced fresh ginger

Freshly squeezed juice of $1/2$ lime

1 teaspoon cinnamon

1 teaspoon allspice

2 jalapeño chiles, or 1 Scotch bonnet chile, seeded

1 large clove garlic

2 tablespoons soy sauce

3 tablespoons malt vinegar

1 tablespoon brown sugar

1 tablespoon fresh thyme

1 teaspoon salt

$3/4$ pound center-cut pork, cut into 1-inch cubes

10 sugarcane sticks, cut into 8-inch-long pieces

$1/2$ pineapple, peeled, cored, and cut into 1-inch cubes

To make the marinade, place the green onions, ginger, lime juice, cinnamon, allspice, chiles, garlic, soy sauce, vinegar, sugar, thyme, and salt in a food processor and blend thoroughly. In a medium bowl, submerge the pork in the marinade, cover, and refrigerate for a minimum of 2 hours.

Oil a barbecue grill and preheat to medium-high. Cut the sugarcane pieces lengthwise into quarters to make thin skewers. Cut one end of each piece at an angle to create a sharp point. Remove the pork from the marinade and thread a piece onto the sugarcane "skewer," followed by a pineapple cube. Repeat so there are two pork cubes and two pineapple cubes on each skewer. Place the skewers on the grill and cook until the meat is brown on all sides, approximately 5 minutes.

VARIATION: *Use chicken or beef instead of pork.*

SPICY TARO CHIPS

MAKES 6 TO 7 CUPS

Salty, slightly spicy, with a denser crunch than you find in commercial chips, these Jamaican chips are addictive. Don't be intimidated by the taro; it's a knobby root vegetable that I found even in a rural New England grocery store. Taro is also known as *tannia* in the British Virgin Islands and on Nevis, *malanga* on Cuba, and *yautia* in Puerto Rico.

> 2 tablespoons salt
> 2 tablespoons chili powder
> 2 tablespoons ground coriander
> 2 tablespoons ground cumin
> Vegetable oil, for frying
> 2 large taros (approximately 3 pounds)
> 1 cup malt vinegar (optional)

Mix the salt, chili powder, coriander, and cumin in a small bowl to form the seasoning. Set aside. In a large saucepan, heat 2 inches of oil to 375°F (medium-high heat). Peel the taros and slice them as thinly as possible. Fry the slices in 2 batches until light brown, approximately 8 to 12 minutes. Using a slotted spoon, transfer the chips to paper towels to drain. While the chips are still hot, sprinkle with the seasoning and toss to coat. Serve with malt vinegar, for dipping.

TUNA CEVICHE

MAKES 20 TO 24 HORS D'OEUVRES

This recipe has a little heat, a little sweet, and a lot of flavor. The acidity of the lime "cooks" the tuna and firms up the flesh.

> 6 ounces yellowfin tuna, ahi, or any pink to red tuna, cut into large dice
> 1 tablespoon minced green onions
> 1 tablespoon diced red bell pepper
> 1 tablespoon chopped fresh cilantro
> 1 tablespoon diced mango
> 2 tablespoons freshly squeezed orange juice
> $1/2$ teaspoon grated orange peel
> 2 tablespoons freshly squeezed lime juice
> $1/2$ teaspoon Scotch bonnet or habanero chile, seeded
> Salt and pepper to taste
> Fried plantain, banana chips or coconut chips

Combine the tuna, green onion, bell pepper, cilantro, mango, orange juice, orange peel, lime juice, and chile. Season with salt and pepper. Cover and refrigerate for 30 minutes. Serve atop fried plantain, banana chips, coconut chips, or tortillas.

CONCH FRITTERS WITH KEY LIME REMOULADE

MAKES 15 FRITTERS

Conch (sometimes called "hurricane ham" because it was all people could find to eat after a big storm) is the heart of Bahamian cuisine. Even Columbus harvested conch off the coast of Cuba on his second voyage. Don't be dissuaded from trying this recipe because of the conch; ask the seafood person at your supermarket, and you may be surprised. You can serve these fritters with either the Key Lime Remoulade or a hot sauce. It's okay to use regular limes instead of key limes.

KEY LIME REMOULADE

3 egg yolks

1 tablespoon grated or finely chopped Key lime peel

3 tablespoons freshly squeezed Key lime juice

1 teaspoon salt

$1/2$ teaspoon pepper

$1^1/4$ cups canola oil

$1/2$ teaspoon Tabasco sauce or other Louisiana-style hot pepper sauce

1 tablespoon minced shallot

1 tablespoon drained capers

1 tablespoon finely chopped cornichons

FRITTERS

5 ounces conch meat

$1/4$ red bell pepper, minced

2 tablespoons minced green onions

1 clove garlic, minced

$1/2$ teaspoon minced seeded Scotch bonnet chile

$1/2$ teaspoon minced fresh ginger

2 tablespoons chopped fresh cilantro

2 tablespoons butter, melted

$3/4$ cup flour

$3/4$ teaspoon baking powder

Canola oil, for frying

$3/4$ cup milk or half-and-half

Salt

To make the remoulade, blend the egg yolks, lime peel, lime juice, salt, and pepper in a food processor or blender. Slowly add the oil, first a few drops at a time and then in a slow stream, until all the oil is incorporated and the sauce is thick. Stir in the Tabasco, shallot, capers, and cornichons. Cover and refrigerate. (The remoulade can be made several days ahead and kept chilled.)

To make the fritters, place the conch between 2 sheets of waxed paper on a flat surface and pound with a cleaver, mallet, or rolling pin. Once tenderized, place conch in food processor and pulse until finely chopped. In a medium bowl, combine the conch, bell pepper, green onions, garlic, chile, ginger, cilantro, and butter. In another bowl, combine the flour and baking powder.

Heat 3 inches of oil in a deep pan to 375°F. Stir the flour mixture into the conch mixture. Add the milk to form a batter. Drop the fritter mixture by tablespoonfuls into the hot oil and cook until they are golden brown on all sides, approximately 3 minutes. Using a slotted spoon, transfer to paper towels to drain. Season with salt.

"I don't want a White Christmas with plenty of snow
I want a bright Christmas with rum and calypso!"
—The Great John L.

CHICKEN AND CHORIZO CROQUETAS WITH SPICY ORANGE EMULSION

MAKES 25 CROQUETAS

Originally from Spain, where they are served hot as tapas, *croquetas* are popular in Spanish communities from Miami to Cuba. You'll find them everywhere, from walk-up counters to bakeries.

SPICY ORANGE EMULSION

1 shallot, peeled

1/2 teaspoon plus 1 cup olive oil

Salt and pepper

1 dried chipotle chile

1/2 cup boiling water

2 cups freshly squeezed orange juice

3 tablespoons cider vinegar

1 teaspoon Dijon mustard

1 teaspoon chili powder

CROQUETAS

2 poblano chiles

2 cups milk

3 tablespoons butter

1/2 cup flour, plus 1/4 cup for dredging

4 ounces chorizo sausage, chopped

4 ounces skinless boneless chicken breast, cooked and diced

2 tablespoons chopped fresh cilantro

1 ear of corn, cooked and kernels removed

1 tablespoon cumin seeds

1 cup bread crumbs or panko (see page 84)

2 eggs, beaten

Canola oil, for frying

1/2 teaspoon salt

To make the emulsion, preheat the oven to 400°F. Lightly coat the peeled shallot with 1/2 teaspoon of the oil. Season with salt and pepper. Place in a small baking dish and roast for 15 to 20 minutes, or until golden. Let cool. Place the chile in a measuring cup and add 1/2 cup boiling water. Let stand 20 minutes, or until softened. Remove the chile from the water and cool.

Heat the orange juice and simmer over medium-low heat until reduced by half, about 20 minutes. Cool. Combine the orange syrup, vinegar, shallot, mustard, chili powder, and chile in a blender or food processor and blend for 1 minute. With the motor running, add the remaining 1 cup oil slowly in a thin stream. Season with salt and pepper. (The emulsion can be made a day ahead.) Cover and refrigerate.

To make the *croquetas,* roast the chiles over a gas flame or under a broiler, turning several times, until they are charred all over. Transfer the chiles to a bowl, cover with plastic wrap, and let steam for 15 minutes. Peel, devein, and seed the chiles, then chop.

In a small saucepan, heat the milk until bubbles appear around the edges. In a large saucepan over medium heat, melt the butter. When the butter is melted, slowly add $1/2$ cup of the flour and cook, whisking constantly, about 2 minutes. Slowly add the warm milk, whisking constantly until smooth. Cook the mixture, whisking frequently, for 5 minutes (the mixture should be thick). Fold the chorizo, chicken, cilantro, chopped chiles, and corn into the mixture. Transfer to a 8 by 8-inch square cake pan. Cover with plastic wrap, pressing wrap against the surface of the mixture, and cool in the refrigerator for at least 6 hours and up to 24 hours.

Place the cumin seeds in a small skillet and toast over medium heat, tossing often, until lightly browned and fragrant, about 3 to 5 minutes. Combine the seeds and bread crumbs in a shallow bowl. Place the beaten eggs in a second shallow bowl, and the remaining $1/4$ cup of flour in a third.

Remove the *croqueta* mixture from the refrigerator and cut into 25 squares. Dredge the *croquetas* in flour, then eggs, and finally the bread crumb mixture. Heat $1/2$ inch of oil in a large, heavy pot to 375°F (medium-high). Fry *croquetas* 4 to 5 minutes, until browned. Using a slotted spoon, transfer the *croquetas* to paper towels to drain. Season with salt. Serve with the Spicy Orange Emulsion.

VARIATION: *Chorizo may be replaced with tasso ham.*

PALM HEARTS SALAD

SERVES 4 TO 6 AS AN APPETIZER

Heart of palm is the tender center of the cabbage palm. It looks like white asparagus, and is considered a delicacy.

> 1 (12-ounce) can whole hearts of palm, thinly sliced lengthwise
>
> 1 avocado, peeled, pitted, and thinly sliced
>
> 1 large carrot, cut in half crosswise and then cut lengthwise into long matchsticks
>
> 2 oranges, skin sliced off and divided into segments
>
> $^1/_2$ large red onion, thinly sliced
>
> 4 cups (loosely packed) watercress, large stems removed
>
> 3 tablespoons freshly squeezed orange juice
>
> 2 tablespoons cider vinegar
>
> Salt and pepper

In a large bowl, gently combine the hearts of palm, avocado, carrot, orange segments, onion, and watercress. In a small bowl, combine the orange juice, vinegar, salt, and pepper. Add the dressing to the salad and toss. Serve immediately.

"High-yellow of my heart, with breasts like tangerines,
You taste better to me than eggplant stuffed with crab,
You are the tripe in my pepper-pot, the dumpling in my peas,
   my tea of aromatic herbs.
You are the corned beef whose customhouse is my heart,
My mush with syrup that trickles down my throat.
You are a steaming dish, mushroom cooked with rice, crisp potato fries,
   and little fish fried brown . . .
My hankering for love follows you wherever you go.
Your bum is a gorgeous basket brimming with fruits and meat."
            —Haitian poet Emile Roumer, "The Haitian Peasant Declares His Love"

PAPAYA AND LOBSTER SALAD

SERVES 4 AS FIRST COURSE OR 2 TO 3 FOR LUNCH

This salad makes an elegant summer luncheon or a hearty first course. The mayonnaise (slightly puckery from the lime) is a perfect complement to the lobster and papaya. If you can't find Caribbean lobster, substitute Atlantic lobster. According to Columbus's notes, the natives called papaya "fruit of the angels."

1 pound cooked lobster meat (see note below)

1 firm but ripe papaya or mango, peeled and seeded

5 green onions, white part and 1 inch of green part

1 red or yellow bell pepper, seeded

4 tablespoons freshly squeezed lime juice

$^1/_3$ cup mayonnaise

Salt and pepper

1 ripe avocado, peeled and pitted

Chop the lobster meat roughly into bite-size pieces. Cut the papaya, green onions, and bell pepper into narrow strips 2 inches long. In a large nonreactive bowl, combine the lobster, papaya, green onions, bell pepper, lime juice, and mayonnaise and mix well. Season with salt and pepper. Slice the avocado horizontally into thin pieces. Divide the avocado slices among the serving plates, fanning out the slices in the center of each plate. Divide the lobster salad among the plates. Serve immediately.

NOTE: *To cook a live lobster, bring a large pot of water to a rolling boil, drop in the lobster head first and boil until it floats, about 15 minutes. Remove the meat from the shell after it cools.*

CARIBBEAN SAMOSAS WITH COCONUT-GINGER MOJO

MAKES 26 SAMOSAS

A popular snack in India, these tasty little turnovers, filled with sweet potato, curry, and peas, have big flavor. (You can freeze the *samosas* after assembling them and cook them later.) The sauce will get your mojo working. The Scotch bonnet chile pepper (also known on one French island, as Mrs. Jacques's Behind) is extremely hot—take care when you handle the pepper that you don't rub your eye (or other sensitive areas) afterward.

COCONUT-GINGER MOJO

- $^1/_2$ cup shredded unsweetened coconut
- 2 teaspoons minced fresh ginger
- $^1/_2$ cup unsweetened coconut milk
- Freshly squeezed juice of 1 lime
- 3 green onions, minced
- $^1/_2$ teaspoon minced seeded Scotch bonnet chile
- $^1/_2$ teaspoon salt

SAMOSAS

- 2 tablespoons canola or vegetable oil, plus additional oil, for frying
- $^1/_2$ small yellow onion, finely chopped
- $1^1/_2$ teaspoons curry powder
- $^1/_2$ teaspoon ground cumin
- $^1/_2$ teaspoon ground allspice
- $^1/_2$ teaspoon salt
- 2 medium-size sweet potatoes, peeled and cut into $^1/_4$ inch dice
- 1 cup vegetable stock or water
- $^2/_3$ cup fresh or frozen peas
- Salt
- 26 wonton wrappers
- 1 egg beaten with 2 tablespoons water, for egg wash

To make the mojo, mix all the ingredients together in a medium bowl. Set aside.

To make the *samosas*, heat 2 tablespoons of the oil in a heavy medium skillet to medium-high. Add the onion and cook until soft, about 3 minutes.

Decrease heat to medium-low and add the curry powder, cumin, allspice, and salt; cook for 2 minutes, stirring constantly. Add the sweet potatoes and stock and cover. Cook until the sweet potatoes are tender, about 10 to 15 minutes. Uncover and cook until the liquid is absorbed. Stir in the peas and season with salt. Transfer the filling to a bowl and let cool completely.

Place 1 wonton wrapper on a work surface. Place 1 heaping teaspoonful of filling in the center of the wrapper. Using a pastry brush, brush the egg wash around the perimeter of the wrapper and fold the wrapper diagonally in half, pressing the edges to seal. Repeat until all wrappers are filled.

Heat $1/2$ inch of oil in a large saucepan to medium-high. Carefully drop the *samosas,* three or four at a time, into the oil and cook 2 minutes, turning once. *Samosas* should be golden brown. Using a slotted spoon, transfer the *samosas* to paper towels to drain. Serve warm with the Coconut-Ginger Mojo.

"Whenever you lose your energy
We have a good remedy
Blue food with some dumplings
Crab & callaloo
Or ah bake and salt fish
That bound to help you
To put back what you lost
Try a beef roti or ah glass of seamoss
Then is back to party!"
　　　　—Calypso lyrics by Trinidad musician Tambu

PICADILLO EMPANADAS

MAKES 15 EMPANADAS

Popular in Cuba and Puerto Rico (as well as Spain and South America), these pastry turnovers filled with meat are among my favorites—a few of these and a beer make lunch in the tropics. They are great with either the Lime Cream or the Ancho–Black Bean Sauce (see page 104); or make both, and let your guests choose.

DOUGH
1^1/$_2$ cups flour
^{1}/$_2$ teaspoon salt
^{1}/$_2$ cup (1 stick) chilled butter, diced
^{1}/$_2$ cup cold water

FILLING
2 tablespoons vegetable oil
^{1}/$_2$ small onion, chopped
^{1}/$_2$ red or green bell pepper, chopped
1 clove garlic, minced
^{1}/$_2$ teaspoon minced seeded Scotch bonnet chile
1 pound ground beef

^{1}/$_4$ teaspoon cayenne pepper
1 teaspoon salt
2 plum tomatoes, seeded and chopped
^{1}/$_2$ teaspoon ground cumin
^{1}/$_4$ cup currants
2 tablespoons drained capers
^{1}/$_4$ cup chopped green olives
4 ounces farmer's cheese, goat cheese, or ricotta
^{1}/$_2$ cup flour, for dusting
1 egg beaten with 2 tablespoons water, for egg wash
Lime Cream (see opposite)
Ancho–Black Bean Sauce (page 104)

For the dough, combine the flour and salt in the bowl of a food processor. Add the butter and process until the mixture resembles fine crumbs. With the food processor running, add the cold water and pulse until a dough ball forms. Cover the dough in plastic wrap and refrigerate for 45 minutes. (The dough may be held in the refrigerator for several days, but it should be brought to room temperature before rolling out.)

For the filling, heat the oil in a heavy large skillet to medium-high. Add the onion, bell pepper, garlic, and chile. Cook until the vegetables are soft, approximately 5 minutes. Add the beef and cook until lightly browned and cooked through, about 8 to 10 minutes. Add the cayenne, salt, tomatoes, cumin, currants, capers, and olives. Decrease the heat to medium-low, cover the skillet, and cook 10 minutes longer. Place the mixture in a bowl and add the cheese. Mix well.

Preheat the oven to 350°F. Dust a work surface and rolling pin with the flour. Roll out the dough to $1/8$ inch thick. Using a 4-inch-diameter glass or cookie cutter, cut out circles. Place 2 tablespoons of filling in the center of each dough circle. Seal the empanadas by folding in half and pressing the edges. Brush the egg wash over the surfaces of the empanadas. Place the empanadas on a greased baking sheet. Bake 10 to 15 minutes, or until golden brown. Serve with the Lime Cream or Ancho–Black Bean Sauce.

Lime Cream

This sauce works with either the empanadas on opposite page or the *arepas* on page 110.

MAKES 1 CUP

> 1 cup sour cream or crème fraîche
> 2 tablespoons freshly squeezed lime juice
> 1 teaspoon grated lime peel
> 1 teaspoon salt

Combine all of the ingredients and mix well. (Lime Cream can be made 1 day ahead. Cover and refrigerate.)

Ancho-Black Bean Sauce

This sauce can be used with either the empanadas on page 102 or the *arepas* on page 110.

MAKES 1^1/2 CUPS

- 1 cup hot water
- 1 dried ancho chile
- 2 tablespoons vegetable oil
- 1 small yellow onion, chopped
- 1 clove garlic, chopped
- 1 teaspoon cumin
- ^{1}/4 cup tomato puree or tomato sauce
- ^{3}/4 cup vegetable stock or water
- 1 teaspoon honey
- 1 (15-ounce) can black beans, drained
- 2 tablespoons finely chopped fresh cilantro
- 2 tablespoons freshly squeezed lime juice
- Salt

Bring 1 cup of hot water to a boil in a small saucepan. Add the ancho chile, remove from heat, and let sit 30 minutes. Remove the chile from the water. Seed and chop the chile and set aside. Reserve ^{1}/4 cup of the soaking liquid.

Heat the oil in a heavy medium saucepan to medium-high. Add the onion and cook, stirring, until soft, about 3 minutes. Add the garlic and cook for 1 minute. Add the cumin and chile and cook for 1 minute. Add the tomato puree, reserved soaking liquid, stock, and honey. Cook until the sauce is reduced by half.

Blend half of the can of beans and the reduced sauce in a blender or food processor until smooth. Transfer the puree to a bowl and add the remaining beans, the cilantro, and lime juice. Season with salt and mix well. Set aside. (The sauce can be made one day ahead. Cover and refrigerate.)

COCONUT-CRUSTED RED SNAPPER TAMALES

MAKES 8 APPETIZER-SIZE TAMALES

Anguilla is known for its seafood: lobster, yellowtail, and red snapper are caught on local reefs. There's a strong coconut riff going on with the fish here in this Anguillan-inspired recipe. It's fine to substitute tilapia or another thin fish for the red snapper.

> 9 corn husks
>
> $1/2$ cup unsweetened coconut
>
> 3 tablespoons minced green onions
>
> 3 tablespoons minced red onion
>
> 3 tablespoons minced fresh cilantro
>
> 1 clove garlic, minced
>
> $1/2$ teaspoon minced fresh ginger
>
> $1/2$ teaspoon salt
>
> $1/2$ teaspoon minced seeded Scotch bonnet chile
>
> 2 tablespoons freshly squeezed lime juice
>
> 3 tablespoons coconut milk
>
> 1 pound red snapper fillet, skin removed, cut into 8 (2-ounce) pieces
>
> 2 teaspoons butter

Soak the corn husks in hot water for 30 minutes.

Preheat the oven to 350°F. Heat a grill to medium-high. Spread the coconut out on a baking sheet and toast in the oven for 5 minutes or until golden brown. (Watch carefully: coconut burns quickly.) Place the coconut in a mixing bowl. Add the green onions, red onion, cilantro, garlic, ginger, salt, chile, lime juice, and coconut milk. Mix well.

Remove the husks from the water and pat dry. Cut 16 tying strings out of 1 husk. Place 1 piece of fish, skin side down, in the center of a whole corn husk and spread a thick layer of the coconut mixture over it. Dab on $1/4$ teaspoon butter. Roll the cornhusk around the fish and tie with 2 tying strings. Repeat with the remaining fish, coconut mixture, and corn husks. Place the tamales on the grill and cover the grill. Cook 5 minutes and serve.

TOSTONES WITH LIME

MAKES 18 TO 20 TOSTONES

Tostones are fried green plantains. Sister to the banana (but starchier), a plantain gets sweeter as it ripens, and islanders eat them at all stages of ripeness—while green they are fried (to make chips), when ripe (black-skinned) they are baked or fried. These *tostones* have a crispy outside and a soft inside—like some men I know.

> Vegetable oil, for frying
> 3 green plantains, peeled and cut crosswise into 1-inch slices
> 1 lime, halved
> Salt

In a large pot, heat 3 inches of oil to 350°F. Add the plantain slices in batches and fry until golden, approximately 3 to 4 minutes. Using a slotted spoon, transfer the slices to paper towels to drain. When cooled, place the slices between 2 pieces of plastic wrap. Using a heavy skillet, press to flatten the slices to $1/8$ inch. Return the slices to the oil and continue cooking for 3 minutes, or until golden. Using a slotted spoon, transfer the *tostones* to clean paper towels and squeeze the lime halves over. Season with salt.

CHAYOTE SLAW

SERVES 4 AS A SIDE DISH OR APPETIZER

Green and slightly pear-shaped, chayote is a tropical squash-like fruit, also known as *cho-cho* and *christophene*.

1 chayote, peeled and pitted

2 carrots, peeled

$1/2$ regular-size cucumber, peeled and seeded

$1/2$ medium-size red onion, thinly sliced

$1/2$ teaspoon finely minced seeded Scotch bonnet chile

$1/2$ cup julienned jicama (peeled)

3 tablespoons olive oil

$1/4$ cup cider vinegar

2 tablespoons freshly squeezed lime juice

$1/4$ cup lightly packed fresh mint leaves, sliced into narrow strips

Salt and pepper

Cut the chayote, carrot, and cucumber into long, narrow strips. Combine all the ingredients in a large mixing bowl. Let the slaw marinate in the refrigerator for 2 hours before serving.

Culinary Influences

Each island is a unique combination of influences from natives to colonists to slaves and indentured servants. On Vieques, you'll find *asopao, arepas,* and rice and beans; just a few miles away on Virgin Gorda, the Brit invasion is apparent in the mulligatawny soup and curries. Avoid resorts; go where the locals eat, and you'll find culinary influences dating back centuries.

- **Antigua:** British
- **Aruba:** African, Dutch
- **Barbados:** British
- **Bermuda:** British
- **British Virgin Islands:** British
- **Cuba:** Spanish, Creole
- **Curaçao:** Dutch, Indonesian, Chinese, Latin American
- **Dominica:** French, Creole, British
- **Dominican Republic:** Spanish, native Dominican
- **Grenada:** English, French
- **Guadeloupe:** French, Creole
- **Haiti:** French
- **Jamaica:** African, Chinese, British
- **Martinique:** French, Creole
- **Montserrat:** Irish
- **Puerto Rico:** Spanish
- **St. Bart's:** French
- **St. Kitts and Nevis:** French, English, African
- **St. Lucia:** French, English, Creole
- **St. Martin:** Dutch, Indonesian, French
- **Trinidad and Tobago:** Indian, African, Chinese, French, Spanish, British
- **United States Virgin Islands:** English, Danish
- **Vieques and Culebra:** Spanish

AREPAS WITH GOAT CHEESE

MAKES 18 AREPAS

Essentially pancakes with two toppings, these bite-size morsels unfold their flavors as you eat them—there's a hint of lime in the cream, and a suggestion of spice in the beans. These cakes can be made ahead, frozen, and reheated later. The batter may also be frozen and used later.

> 1 pound fresh corn or frozen, thawed corn
> 1¹/2 cups extra-fine yellow cornmeal
> 1 tablespoon sugar
> 2 tablespoons flour
> 4 ounces goat cheese, crumbled
> 1 teaspoon salt
> 3 tablespoons milk
> 1 cup boiling water
> Lime Cream (page 103), for garnish
> Ancho–Black Bean Sauce (page 104), for garnish

Blend the corn in a blender or food processor until coarsely chopped. In a mixing bowl, combine the cornmeal, sugar, flour, cheese, and salt. Stir in the milk. Add the boiling water and mix well.

Lightly coat a griddle with oil and heat to medium. Spoon the batter by heaping tablespoonfuls onto the griddle to form cakes and cook 3 to 4 minutes on each side. Garnish with dollops of lime cream and ancho-black bean sauce.

VARIATION: *Monterey Jack cheese may be substituted for the goat cheese.*

GRILLED OYSTERS WITH TWO SAUCES

MAKES 24 OYSTERS

I love Puerto Rico and its sister, Vieques. Along their highways and backroads you find many *lechonerias* (outdoor barbecue stalls), where you might see *lechón asado* (roasted pig) next to an active vodoun shrine that the chef's working on when he has no customers. Puerto Rico is also renowned for its mangrove oysters, which are small and sweet. Away from the mangrove swamps they're hard to find, so any small oyster will work in this recipe. Shucking oysters is a pain in the neck. If you want to say shuck it, you can put them on the grill whole (see the instructions below). The shucked oysters will yield a slightly smokier flavor, but either way, the taste is awesome. The versatile Caribbean-style hot sauce here can also be used for dipping bammies, fritters, and other foods.

VANILLA-RUM BUTTER

$1/2$ cup (1 stick) unsalted butter, room temperature

$1/2$ tablespoon dark rum

$1/2$ shallot, minced

1 vanilla bean

SWEET AND FIERY PAPAYA SAUCE

$1^1/2$ cups papaya puree (from about $1^1/2$ ripe papayas)

1 tablespoon minced red onion

1 Scotch bonnet chile, seeded and chopped

1 plum tomato, seeded and chopped

$1/2$ teaspoon minced fresh ginger

1 tablespoon rice vinegar

2 teaspoons sugar

2 tablespoons freshly squeezed lime juice

1 tablespoon tomato puree or tomato sauce

$1/4$ cup water

1 teaspoon salt

OYSTERS

24 oysters, shucked (shucked oysters may be kept in the refrigerator, covered with a wet towel, for up to one hour)

To make the vanilla-rum butter, combine the butter, rum, and shallot in a small saucepan over medium heat. Warm until the butter is melted. Slice the vanilla bean lengthwise in half and scrape the seeds into the butter mixture. Stir and heat for 2 minutes. Keep melted and warm for serving.

To make the hot sauce, blend all the ingredients in a food processor for 2 minutes. Place the purée in a medium saucepan and cook over medium heat for 10 minutes.

To make the oysters, preheat the grill to medium-high. Place the shucked oysters on the grill. Cover the grill and cook until the oysters are plump and their edges start to curl, about 4 minutes. (If you choose not to shuck, put the oysters in their shell on the grill, rounded side down, and cover the grill, cooking until they open, about 5 minutes. Discard any oysters that do not open.) Serve the oysters in the shell, with both sauces on the side.

Authentic Caribbean Hot Sauces

Matouk's (Trinidad)

Windmill (Barbados)

Spitfire Barbados Hot Pepper Sauce (Barbados)

Pickapeppa Sauce (Jamaica)

Erica's Country-Style Pepper Sauce (St. Vincent)

Busha Browne's Pukka Sauce (Jamaica)

Grand Anse Moko Jumbie (St. Thomas)

Outerbridge's Sherry Pepper Sauce (Bermuda)

Sunny Caribbee Hot Sauce (Tortola)

Miss Anna's Hot Pepper "The Appetite Food" Sauce (St. Croix)

Chief Trinidad Hot Sauce (Trinidad)

Marinda's West Indian Hot Sauce (St. Vincent)

ROTI WITH DILL-MINT CHUTNEY

MAKES 16 ROTI

Roti is an Indian snack that is popular in the southern Caribbean, especially Trinidad. In 1844 the British began to bring indentured servants from India, and by 1870, forty thousand Indians were living in Trinidad. At the end of their five-year servitude, the servants had the choice of a free passage home or a plot of land in Trinidad. Today the Indian influence is everywhere—from the Hindu temples and Muslim festivals to curry-laced street food. Roti vendors are on many street corners all over the island, selling this fragrant bread stuffed with chickpeas, potato, pumpkin, chicken, or fish.

DILL-MINT CHUTNEY

$1/4$ cup chopped onion

$1^1/2$ cups (lightly packed) stemmed fresh dillweed

1 cup (lightly packed) stemmed fresh mint

1 tablespoon minced fresh ginger

1 clove garlic, chopped

2 jalapeño chiles, seeded and chopped

1 teaspoon sugar

$1/2$ teaspoon salt

3 tablespoons white vinegar

$1/2$ cup plain yogurt

DOUGH

3 cups flour

1 teaspoon baking powder

2 teaspoon salt

2 tablespoons canola oil

$1/3$ cup (or more) water

FILLING

1 tablespoon canola oil

2 cloves garlic, minced

Pinch of saffron

1 teaspoon ground cumin

2 cups drained canned chickpeas (garbanzo beans)

$1/2$ cup water

Salt and pepper

Flour, for dusting

1 tablespoon butter, melted, cooled

To make the chutney, place all the ingredients in a food processor and blend until smooth. (The chutney can be made a day ahead. Cover and refrigerate.)

To make the dough, combine the flour, baking powder, and salt in a food processor. With the motor running, add the oil and enough water to form the dough. Transfer to a bowl and let rest for 15 minutes.

Meanwhile, make the filling: In a sauté pan, heat the oil over medium heat. Add the garlic and saffron and cook 1 minute. Add the cumin, chickpeas, water, and salt. Simmer until all the water has evaporated. Season with salt and pepper. Cool to lukewarm and purée in a food processor. Set aside.

Form 16 balls from the dough and let rest 5 more minutes. Make a well in the center of each ball. Drop 2 teaspoons of filling into the hole and press the dough around the filling to enclose. Using your palm and fingertips or a rolling pin, flatten each ball on a floured surface to a 4-inch disk. Brush with melted butter. Lightly coat a griddle with oil and heat to medium. Working in batches, cook the rotis on 1 side for 3 minutes. Brush the top with butter, turn over, and cook for 2 minutes longer. Transfer to a platter. Serve warm with the chutney.

SEA SCALLOPS WITH SWEET POTATO-PLANTAIN HASH AND PINEAPPLE VINAIGRETTE

SERVES 4 AS AN APPETIZER

Caribbean sea scallops, called calico scallops, are smaller than those found in the Atlantic. For this Cuban–Key West recipe, any type of scallop will do. The zesty vinaigrette is also good drizzled over other types of seafood, or vegetables such as asparagus and broccoli.

PEPPERED PINEAPPLE VINAIGRETTE

1 cup cubed pineapple

Canola oil

Salt and coarsely ground black pepper

$1/4$ shallot, minced

2 tablespoons cider vinegar

$1/2$ teaspoon Dijon mustard

$1/2$ cup olive oil

HASH AND SCALLOPS

2 tablespoons canola oil

$1/3$ cup diced salt pork

$1/2$ cup diced onion

$1/2$ cup diced peeled sweet potato

$1/2$ cup diced peeled white-skinned potato

$1/4$ cup water or vegetable stock

$1/2$ ripe plantain, peeled and diced

$1/4$ cup frozen corn kernels, thawed

3 green onions, white and light green parts only, chopped, plus 1 green onion sliced into narrow strips, for garnish

Salt and pepper

12 sea scallops

Coat the pineapple lightly with canola oil, then season lightly with salt and generously with coarsely ground black pepper. Heat sauté pan to medium-high. When the pan is hot, add the pineapple and cook for 5 minutes. Remove from heat and let cool. In a food processor, blend the pineapple, shallot, vinegar, and mustard for 1 minute. With the motor running, slowly add the olive oil in a thin stream. Season with salt and set aside.

To make the hash, heat 1 tablespoon of the oil in a sauté pan. Add the salt pork and diced onion and cook until the onion is soft. Add both types of potatoes and the water or stock and cook until all the liquid evaporates. Add the plantain, corn, and the 3 chopped green onions, cooking for 2 minutes longer. Season with salt and pepper.

Preheat the oven to 400°F. Heat a sauté pan to medium-high and add the remaining 1 tablespoon of oil. Gently pat the scallops dry with a paper towel and season with salt and pepper. Sear the scallops in the pan until golden brown on both sides, approximately 1 to 2 minutes per side. Transfer the scallops to a baking sheet and bake in the oven for 3 minutes.

Place $1/2$ cup of hash on each of 4 plates. Place 3 scallops on top of the hash on each plate. Drizzle 1 tablespoon of the vinaigrette lightly over the scallops and around each plate. Garnish with the green onion strips.

"Every tree is pleasant to the sight and good for food."
—Columbus, sailing by Trinidad

RICE AND PIGEON-PEAS CAKES WITH CILANTRO-PEPPER PESTO

MAKES 24 TO 30 HORS D'OEUVRES

Originally from West Africa, pigeon peas are a staple of Caribbean cooking, especially rice dishes. They're also known as gungo peas, goongoo peas, or congo beans. You'll find them in Caribbean or Latin American markets, or in the Latin American section of some supermarkets.

PESTO

1/4 cup chopped yellow onion

2 cloves garlic

2 tablespoons grated Parmesan cheese

1 poblano chile, seeded and chopped

1 bunch fresh cilantro with stems

1 tablespoon minced fresh ginger

2 tablespoons pumpkin seeds (pepitas)

2 tablespoons extra-virgin olive oil

2 tablespoons freshly squeezed lime juice

1 teaspoon salt

RICE CAKES

2 cups water

1 teaspoon salt

1 cup white rice

3/4 cup drained canned pigeon peas

2 eggs, beaten

1/2 cup flour

3 tablespoons canola oil

Lime Cream (optional; page 103)

To make the pesto, place all ingredients in a food processor. Blend well, occasionally scraping down the sides of the bowl. Set aside.

To make the rice cakes, place the water and salt in saucepan and bring to a boil. Add the rice. Cover the pan and reduce heat to low. Cook 20 minutes or until all water is absorbed. Turn off the stove and let the rice cool. (The cakes are easier to form if the rice is slightly overcooked.) Add the pigeon peas and eggs.

Add $^1/_4$ cup plus 2 tablespoons of the pesto to the rice mixture. Mix well and refrigerate until chilled, about 1 to 2 hours.

Place the flour on a plate. Using 1 tablespoonful of the rice mixture, form 1 cake. Repeat with remaining rice mixture. Coat the cakes lightly with flour and flatten into disk shapes. Heat the oil in a sauté pan to medium-high. Working in batches, add the cakes and cook 2 minutes, or until bottoms are golden brown. Turn and cook another 2 minutes. Transfer to paper towels to drain. Serve immediately with the remaining pesto or lime cream.

VARIATION: *The rice mixture may be used as a stuffing for tomatoes or bell peppers.*

Names for Islands

Explorers were food-inspired when they mapped out names for Caribbean inlets and islands as evidenced by the following food on the charts.

Prickly Pear	Salt Island	Rum Cay
Great Carrot Bay	Ginger Island	Muskmelon Bay
Watermelon Cay	Carrot Rock	Apple Bay
Cinnamon Cay		

ISLANDTIMELINE

1492: Columbus lands in the West Indies and claims several islands for Spain; a year later he introduces sugarcane to Hispaniola

1503: African slaves brought to Hispaniola by Spanish settlers

1507: Important atlas map produced, naming the New World "America" after Amerigo Vespucci

1518: Large slave uprising in Hispaniola

1562: Funded by Queen Elizabeth, Englishman John Hawkins brings three hundred slaves to Hispaniola from West Africa and trades them to the Spanish for sugar, ginger, and pearls. (Two years later, Hawkins introduces tobacco to England from Florida.)

1500s–1700s: Golden age of piracy

1611: Shakespeare writes *The Tempest,* based on William Strachey's 1609 account of being shipwrecked on Bermuda

1640–1680: Large-scale slave labor imported to the British Caribbean

1655: Jamaica becomes a British colony

1703: Rum is made commercially on Barbados (at Mount Gay)

1719: Daniel Defoe writes *Robinson Crusoe* about the "Caribbee Islands"

1760: Tacky's Rebellion, a large slave revolt in Jamaica

1780: Massachusetts constitution declares that "all men are born free and equal"

1788: Captain Bligh brings breadfruit to Jamaica aboard the HMS *Bounty*

1791: Santo Domingo revolt (ten thousand slaves killed)

1836: Slavery abolished in the English colonies, including Trinidad, Tobago, and Barbados

1885: Winslow Homer arrives in the Caribbean

1896: The daiquiri invented in Cuba

1920: Prohibition becomes law in the United States

1924: Alec Waugh (brother of Evelyn) has the first "cocktail party"

1934: Prohibition repealed

1959: Cuba, which gave us the Cuba libre, the daiquiri, and the mojito, sees Castro rise to power in the revolution of 1959

CARIBBEANCOCKTAILS MOVIES

Captain Blood, 1935. This high-seas adventure film begins in 1685, when King James II deports Erroll Flynn's character from England to Jamaica to be a slave. This is the pirate flick that launched Erroll Flynn's career as a swashbuckler.

Carnival of Souls, 1962. Haitian voodoo cult classic.

Cocktail, 1988. Set in Jamaica, a thin movie starring Tom Cruise as bartender. But there's some wonderful Jamaican scenery and a memorable soundtrack, including Bobby McFerrin's "Don't Worry, Be Happy" and the Beach Boys' "Kokomo."

Cool Runnings, 1993. Surprise hit comedy featuring John Candy as coach of the Jamaican Olympics bobsled team (they practiced on a bobsled with wheels). True story.

The Deep, 1977. A scuba thriller about a couple on holiday in Bermuda, based on a novel by *Jaws* author Peter Benchley. Directed by Peter Yates, featuring spectacular underwater photography and, of course, Jacqueline Bissett in a wet T-shirt.

Florida Straits, 1986. Fred Ward and Raul Julia in a Cuban-Caribbean adventure.

The Harder They Come, 1973. Gritty cult film starring Jimmy Cliff as a renegade musician, with a soundtrack by Jimmy Cliff (*Sitting in Limbo,* etc.)—a classic!

A High Wind in Jamaica, 1965. Anthony Quinn in a classic pirate flick, from the eerie novel by Richard Hughes.

The Island, 1979. Goofy adventure flick with an absurd plot, starring Michael Caine as a kidnap victim to a "lost" band of pirates.

James Bond. Many island tales *(Dr. No, Thunderball, Never Say Never Again)* based in the Caribbean, with lots of great island scenes from the '60s.

The Mighty Quinn, 1989. Set in Jamaica, a thriller about a police chief accused of killing a businessman. Early film appearances for Denzel Washington and Robert Townsend.

92° in the Shade, 1976. A cool movie about warring fishing guides in the Florida Keys, featuring Peter Fonda, Warren Oates, and Burgess Meredith. First directorial effort by novelist Thomas McGuane.

The Serpent and the Rainbow, 1988. Cult zombie/voodoo flick set in Haiti, directed by horror master Wes Craven.

CARIBBEANCOCKTAILS READINGROOM

Caribbean, by James Michener. The Caribbean gets the Michener treatment with an almost exhausting tale of the islands from the days of the Arawak tribe to modern times.

Don't Stop the Carnival, by Herman Wouk. A must-read for anyone with ambitions of moving to the islands to get away from it all.

Far Tortuga, by Peter Matthiessen. In his distinctive style, with lyrical descriptions of nature and the sea, Matthiessen tells the tale of a superstitious turtle fisherman on a hunting voyage out from Grand Cayman.

Floridays, by Don Blanding. Lovely, evocative poems singing the praises of a Florida few still remember.

A House for Mr. Biswas, by V. S. Naipaul. An early masterpiece by the Nobel Prize—winning novelist and poet, set in rural Trinidad.

Island in the Sun, by Alec Waugh. A novel (by Evelyn's brother) about colonialism in the West Indies.

Islands in the Stream, by Ernest Hemingway. About an adventurer-painter who travels from Bimini in the '30s to Cuba during World War II. For a complete testosterone-fueled tour of the islands, also read *The Old Man and the Sea* and *To Have and to Have Not.*

Our Man in Havana, by Graham Greene. From this old-school writer of Caribbeana, set in Cuba in the 1950s during the Cold War.

A Small Place, by Jamaica Kincaid. Life in Antigua.

Tales from Margaritaville, by Jimmy Buffett. A tropical tour of the islands in short-story form.

Texaco, by Patrick Chamoiseau. A favorite of many, this novel about 150 years of slavery in Martinique portrays the stark life of a slave.

Treasure Island, by Robert Louis Stevenson. Inspired by Norman Island (in the British Virgin Islands), Stevenson's classic story of adventure, greed, and daring with Long John Silver.

When I Was Puerto Rican, by Esmeralda Santiago. An evocative coming-of-age memoir about growing up poor in rural Puerto Rico—everything from the sounds of *coqui* at night to how to get a dead baby's soul to heaven.

Where Is Joe Merchant?, by Jimmy Buffett. A wacked-out fictional account of a Harrison Ford–like hero traversing the islands in his seaplane, by the king of laid-back rhythm and song.

The Wide Sargasso Sea, by Jean Rhys. Epic set in Jamaica in the 1830s.

SELECTEDBIBLIOGRAPHY

Callaloo, Calypso, & Carnival, by Dave DeWitt and Mary Jane Wilan. Freedom, California: The Crossing Press, 1993.

The Culinaria Caribbean, by Rosemary Parkinson. Cologne: Konemann, 1999.

The Islands and the Sea, edited by John A. Murray. New York: Oxford University Press, 1991.

Sky Juice and Flying Fish, by Jessica B. Harris. New York: Simon & Schuster, 1991.

Straight Up or On the Rocks, by William Grimes. New York: Simon & Schuster, 1993.

Tequila: In Search of the Blue Agave, by Ian Chadwick. Online: www.ianchadwick.com.

Tropical Bar Book, by Charles Schumann. New York: Stuart, Tabori & Chang, 1986.

Tropical Cocktails, by Barry Shelby. New York: Abbeville Press, 1999.

INDEX

ABOUTTHEAUTHOR

JENNIFER TRAINER THOMPSON is the author of seven books and coauthor of two books ranging in subject from spicy vegetarian cooking to nuclear power. Her articles have appeared in the *New York Times, Travel & Leisure, Diversion, Omni,* and *Harvard.* A James Beard nominee, she is the owner and chef of the Jump Up & Kiss Me brand of food products and a prolific Ten Speed poster producer. Thompson lives with her family in rural Massachusetts, though she can also be spotted in Vieques.

Photo by H. Allen